THE
STATE OF THE WORLD
ATLAS

new revised fifth edition

Michael Kidron and Ronald Segal

PENGUIN
REFERENCE

PENGUIN BOOKS

Published by the Penguin Group
Penguin Books Limited, 27 Wrights Lane,
London W8 5TZ, England
Penguin USA Inc., 375 Hudson Street,
New York, New York 10014, USA
Penguin Books Australia Limited,
Ringwood, Victoria, Australia
Penguin Books Canada Limited, 10 Alcorn Avenue,
Toronto, Ontario, Canada M4V 3B2
Penguin Books (NZ) Limited, 182–190 Wairau Road,
Auckland 10, New Zealand
Penguin Books Limited, Registered Offices:
Harmondsworth, Middlesex, England

First published 1995
10 9 8 7 6 5 4 3 2 1

Text:
Copyright © Michael Kidron and Ronald Segal, 1995
Maps and graphics:
Copyright © Myriad Editions Limited, 1995
All rights reserved

The moral right of the authors has been asserted

Produced for the Penguin Group by
Myriad Editions Limited, 32 Hanway Street,
London WIP 9DD

Edited and co-ordinated for Myriad Editions by
Anne Benewick and Candida Lacey
Graphic design by Corinne Pearlman
Text design by Pentagram Design Limited
Maps created by Angela Wilson for
Line + Line Limited, Thames Ditton, Surrey

Printed and bound in Hong Kong
Produced by Mandarin Offset Limited

CONTENTS

This fifth edition of the atlas records considerable changes. The end of the Soviet Union has led to a number of successor states, with little evidence that the lives of many citizens have been enhanced in consequence. The former satellites, those so-called people's democracies which were so conspicuously neither popular nor democratic, have gone their various ways: East Germany, for instance, to reunification with the West; Czechoslovakia to a division whose benefits appear as elusive as its purposes appeared unwholesome to outsiders; and Yugoslavia, that early breakaway satellite, to a fragmentation whose rival nationalisms have added 'ethnic cleansing' to the language of contemporary politics.

If much may seem to have changed, much has stayed the same or become simply more so. Ever more secure in its power and authority is a business culture whose boards of management pay small regard to the sovereignty of the state except to exploit it. The market is exalted as the dynamic of personal freedom and social endeavour, and the marketplace is increasingly global in its operations. Within this ascendancy, what is considered legitimate business has both a colleague and a competitor in organized crime: both recognize frontiers only in contriving how to cross them; both measure success or failure only by the bottom line. Indeed, in Russia, Ukraine and other successor states of the former USSR, such crime seems to be beating legitimate business at its own game.

Within the rich states of established parliamentary institutions, the concentration of power has proceeded apace, with sharpening economic inequalities in many of them. An increasing government impatience towards the victims of the process is revealed in state erosions of social welfare, as an increasing repressiveness looks to the building of still more prisons. What was once among the rich states a commitment, albeit largely rhetorical, to provide aid for economic development in the poor states, is now a concern for tighter immigration controls to keep the wretched of the earth in their place. Only for migrating capital is there always an asylum.

There is an exposed nerve in the system, however, and the pain that it generates grows and spreads, despite attempts to deny or belittle it. The convenience of driving a car wherever you please does not cancel the distress of watching your own children struggle with asthma. Reports of global warming become less alarmist and more alarming when freak weather patterns assail your own neighbourhood. The strictest of immigration controls are useless against the emissions of greenhouse gases half a world away. When the bosses of the insurance

business become ecologists, the crisis has moved beyond
the apostles of alternative lifestyles.

The approaching end of the millennium looks set to be
accompanied by apocalyptic visions, which may find
evidence enough in our atlas to sustain them. We remain
sanguine all the same, if only because with every day
that passes, the posturings and preoccupations, the
divisiveness and danger, the essential disorderliness of
competing states, appear more absurd. We are well
aware that any call to a united human community brings
the pat reply that this is unreal. Yet, surely, what is far
more unreal, or should be, is that innumerable children
are killed or maimed by landmines laid in some past or
present war; that supposedly allied states turn upon one
another over who should still further deplete the already
dying sea of its fish; that humanity is busily choking on
its own fumes. Our case rests.

We thank in the acknowledgements various people for
the help they have so readily given us. We take pleasure
in expressing here our gratitude to the editorial team at
Myriad – Anne Benewick, Candida Lacey and Corinne
Pearlman – for spurring us into increasing our pace when
our energy flagged and for reining in our zeal when it
threatened to run away with us. Above all, we thank
each other, for one more episode in a collaboration that
has withstood fifteen years of ageing, but whose spirit is
constantly rejuvenated by a shared sense of fun as well
as of purpose.

Michael Kidron
Ronald Segal

ACKNOWLEDGEMENTS

The authors would like to thank the following people for their help in connection with:

4 The Guzzlers (energy) : Fred Dixon, World Energy Council, London.

5 Infernal Combustion (vehicles): Roger Mackett, Centre for Transport Studies, University of London; John Pulak, Transport Studies Unit, Oxford University; Peter White, Transport Studies Group, University of Westminster, London; Chris Batten, Andrea Lannon and Martin Rafferty, Department of Transport, London; Helen Berry, The Chartered Institute of Transport, London; and, Richard Watkins, The Highways Agency, London.

8 Diasporas: Professor Bhikhu Parekh of Hull University.

13 Connections (telecommunications): Emma Jackets and Lydia Jacobson, International Institute of Communications, London; Enzo Paci, World Tourist Office, Madrid; Dave Taylor, Office of Telecommunications (Oftel), London; and, Gregory Staple and Zachary Schrag, Telegeography Inc., Washington, D.C.

16 Missing Women (women's rights): Janet Gormek, Salim Johan and Inge Kaul at the Human Development Report office, UNDP, New York; Joann Vanek, at the UN Statistical Office, New York; Ann Hennan and Andrea Subhan, at the European Parliamentary Committee on Women's Rights office, Luxembourg; Lesley Mitchell, Association of Female Barristers, London; and, Sally Boden and Naila Kabeer, Institute of Development Studies, University of Sussex.

18 Child Exploitation (child labour): Bernie Russell, 'Free Labour World', Brussels.

19 The Killing Weed (tobacco): George Gay, World Tobacco, Redhill, Surrey; Alan Lopez, World Health Organization, Geneva; Judith Mackay, Asian Consultancy on Tobacco Control, Hong Kong; Bill Marks, U.S. Center for Disease Control, Office on Smoking and Health, Atlanta, Georgia; Richard Peto, Radcliffe Infirmary, Oxford; and, Nicholas Wald, St Bartholomew's Hospital Medical College, London.

20 Plagues New and Renewed (AIDS and tuberculosis): Dr Paul Akibumi Sato of the WHO Global Programme on AIDS and Mrs Kathleen Canon of the WHO Tuberculosis Programme.

23 The Labour Force: John Svenningsen, Director of the Bureau for Workers' Activities, and his colleague, Coen Daman, as well as other experts in the International Labour Office, Geneva.

27 Hedges and Bets (financial markets): the librarians of the Reference Library, U.S. Embassy, London.

28 The Golden Fix (narcotics): Ann Girvan, U.S. Reference Center, London.

29 Privatization: Rodney Lord, Privatisation International, London and Charles Vuylsteke, European Bank for Reconstruction and Development, London.

31 Notional Income (purchasing power): Alan Heston, Professor of Economics, University of Pennsylvania; Melinda Limjap, Division of Information, Bureau for Resources and Special Activities, United Nations, New York; Alexandra McLeod, UN Information Centre, London; and, Sarus Menon and Laura Mourino, Office of the Human Development Report, United Nations Development Program, New York.

39 Under Arms (the armed forces): Jennifer Bond, National Science Foundation, Washington, D.C.; Howard Clark, War Resisters' International, London.

40 State Terror (capital punishment and torture): Elana Dallas, Amnesty International, and Amanda Smith at the Death Penalty Information Center, Washington, D.C.

41 Smoking Guns (war and peace): Dan Smith, International Peace Research Institute (PRIO), Oslo.

42 God and Caesar (religion); Martin Palmer and Joanne O'Brien, International Consultancy on Religion, Education and Culture, Manchester.

45 Refugee Makers (refugees): Ginny Hamilton, U.S. Committee for Refugees, Washington, D.C.

47 The Three Monkeys (censorship): Philip Spender and Irena Maryniak, Index on Censorship, London.

48 Tongue-tied (language): Donald Kenrick, London, and Erik Gunnemark, Gothenburg.

50 Addition and Division (states): Alexandra McLeod, UN Information Centre, London; Carol Priestly and other staff at the Foreign and Commonwealth Office, London; and, staff at the Library, Chatham House (The Royal Institute of International Affairs), London.

The graphic lists reported fatal radiation accidents or incidents connected with nuclear power plants and laboratories between 1945 and 1992. They range from deaths caused by the theft of radioactive material to those resulting from the major nuclear reactor accident at Chernobyl in 1986.

This tells only part of the story. In 1994, the World Health Organisation reported a substantial and continuing increase in childhood thyroid cancer in Belarus, Russia and Ukraine following the Chernobyl disaster.

Fatal accidents at military installations are not included.

Sources: International Atomic Energy Agency;
Nuclear Engineering International.

Los Alamos, U.S.A. 1945
Los Alamos, U.S.A. 1946
Vinca, Yugoslavia 1958
Los Alamos, U.S.A. 1958
Idaho Falls, U.S.A. 1961
Woods River, U.S.A. 1964
Switzerland n.d.
Mexico City, Mexico n.d.
West Germany n.d.
Rhode Island, U.S.A. n.d.
Brescia, Italy 1975
Oklahoma, U.S.A. n.d.
Algeria n.d.
Norway n.d.
Constituentes, Argentina 1983
Morocco n.d.
Chernobyl, Ukraine 1986
Goiania, Brazil n.d.
Xin Zhou, China 1992

GREENLAND
(Den)

ICELAND

CANADA

10%
UNITED KINGDOM
IRELAND
NORWAY
SWEDEN
DENMARK
GERMANY
CZECH
AUS

UNITED STATES
OF AMERICA

PORTUGAL

MALTA 4

BERMUDA

13%
ALGERIA

11%

LIB

MEXICO

BAHAMAS

17%

WESTERN SAHARA
MAURITANIA

CUBA

36%

DOMINICAN
REPUBLIC

ATLANTIC
OCEAN

CAPE VERDE

10%

23%
MALI

12%

11%
NIGER

BELIZE
GUATEMALA
EL SALVADOR
HONDURAS
JAMAICA
HAITI

23%

NICARAGUA

COSTA RICA

PANAMA

VENEZUELA

GUYANA

BARBADOS

17%

TRINIDAD & TOBAGO

SENEGAL
GAMBIA
GUINEA-BISSAU
GUINEA
SIERRA LEONE
LIBERIA
CÔTE d'
IVOIRE
BURKINA
FASO
BENIN
GHANA
TOGO
NIGERIA
CAMEROON
EQUATORIAL GUINEA
GABON
CONGO

PACIFIC
OCEAN

SURINAME
FRENCH GUIANA (Fr)

COLOMBIA

ECUADOR

10%
BRAZIL

ANG

PERU

BOLIVIA

PARAGUAY

CHILE

NAMIB

URUGUAY

ARGENTINA

PROPORTION OF LAND AREA SUBJECT TO
HIGH HUMAN DISTURBANCE
from permanent agricultural or
urban development, soil degradation,
and other factors
1993 percentages

THREATENED SPECIES
1990s

10% or over of known mammal
species are threatened

Highest: Madagascar, 48%; Cuba, 36%; Fiji, 25%;
Jamaica, Mauritania, 23%

80%
60%
40%
20%

no data

10% or over of known bird species
are threatened

Highest: Malta, 46%; Kuwait, 26%; Saudi Arabia, 20%

Source: World Resources Institute, *World Resources 1994-95*.

Highest: Denmark, Ireland, 100%; Netherlands, 98%; Burund

14

THREATENED BIRDS *1990s*
percentages of total number of species known
Source: World Resources Institute, *World Resources 1994-95.*

3 countries 15%
8 countries 10%
44 countries
5%
70 countries

"...The sedge is wither'd from the lake,
And no birds sing."
- John Keats

RUSSIA

KAZAKHSTAN

MONGOLIA

10%

CHINA

11%

13%

14%

13%

IRAN

PAKISTAN

NEPAL

BHUTAN

12%

INDIA

14%

MYANMAR

VIETNAM

13%

10%

10%

18%

MALAYSIA

SINGAPORE

N. KOREA

JAPAN 12%

S. KOR

12%

PACIFIC
OCEAN

TAIWAN

HONG KONG

PHILIPPINES

BRUNEI

INDONESIA

PAPUA
NEW
GUINEA

12%

SOLOMON
ISLANDS

AUSTRALIA

14%

25%

FIJI

NEW
ZEALAND

CYPRUS
LEB SYRIA 12%
ISRAEL JOR 11%
IRAQ
KUWAIT
26%
BAHRAIN
QATAR UAE
20%
SAUDI ARABIA
EGYPT 12%
OMAN
13%
IRAN 11%

THREATENED MAMMALS *1990s*
percentages of total number of species known
Source: World Resources Institute, *World Resources 1994-95.*

9 countries 15%
20 countries 10%
64 countries
5%
30 countries

Northwest Territories

C A N A D A

IRELAND

UNITED KINGDOM

NORWAY

SWEDEN

FINLAN

ESTON

LATVI

LITHUANIA

DENMARK

BELA

POLAND

NETH

BEL

GERMANY

CZECH REPUBLIC

SLOVAK

UKRA

FRANCE

SWITZ

AUSTRIA

HUNGARY

ROMA

SLO

CROATIA

B - H

YUG

ITALY

ALB

M

BULG

PORTUGAL

SPAIN

GREECE

California

Mrs

UNITED STATES
OF AMERICA

Mississippi
Basin

MEXICO

CUBA

BAHAMAS

DOMINICAN
REPUBLIC

JAMAICA

HAITI

PUERTO RICO (U.S.)

*ATLANTIC
OCEAN*

MOROCCO

TUNISIA

ALGERIA

LIB

WESTERN SAHARA

BELIZE

GUATEMALA

EL SALVADOR

HONDURAS

NICARAGUA

COSTA RICA

PANAMA

TRINIDAD & TOBAGO

VENEZUELA

GUYANA

SURINAME

FRENCH GUIANA (Fr)

CAPE VERDE

MAURITANIA

MALI

NIGER

SENEGAL

GAMBIA

GUINEA-BISSAU

GUINEA

SIERRA LEONE

LIBERIA

CÔTE d'
IVOIRE

BURKINA
FASO

GHANA

BENIN

TOGO

NIGERIA

CAMEROON

C

EQUATORIAL GUINEA

GABON

CONGO

COLOMBIA

ECUADOR

PERU

B R A Z I L

BOLIVIA

PARAGUAY

CHILE

URUGUAY

ARGENTINA

ANGO

NAMIBI

DISAPPEARING FORESTS
1981-90 annual percentage rates

2% decline in forests

1%

0.5%

marginal or no change

measurable reforestation

no data

Highest deforestation: Jamaica, 5.3%;
Haiti, 3.9%; Bangladesh, 3.3%

**ENVIRONMENTAL DISASTERS CAUSED
BY FREAK WEATHER PATTERNS** *1987-94*

major fires

major storms

drought

floods

coral bleaching due to rise in sea temperature

HAWAII

**STATES REFORESTING AT ANNUAL RATE OF
0.5 PERCENT OR ABOVE** *1981-90*

1.3%

1.1%

0.6%

0.5%

Germany
Hungary
Portugal

Switzerland

UK

Ireland

Sources: Greenpeace, *Climate Time Bomb*, 1994; World
Resources Institute, *World Resources 1994-95*; press reports.

Source: World Resources Institute, *World Resources 1994-95*.

"The fact is that in recent years natural disasters whose return period used to be regarded as at least 100 years have transpired every year in various places in the world. It seems difficult to believe that these incidents are merely accidental." Shiro Horichi, Executive Vice-Pesident, Tokyo Marine and Fire,1993.

RUSSIA

KAZAKHSTAN

MONGOLIA

GEO
AZER
UZBEKISTAN
KIRGISTAN
TURKMEN
TAJ

N KOREA
JAPAN
S KOREA

URKEY

SYRIA
LEB
RAE JOR
IRAQ
IRAN
AFGHANISTAN
CHINA

KUWAIT
BAHRAIN
QATAR
UAE
SAUDI ARABIA
OMAN
YEMEN

PAKISTAN
NEPAL
BHUTAN

PACIFIC
OCEAN

TAIWAN

Straits of
Hormuz
INDIA
MYANMAR
LAOS
VIETNAM

THAILAND
CAM

PHILIPPINES

ERITREA
DJIBOUTI

ETHIOPIA
SOMALIA
SRI LANKA

UGANDA
KENYA
BRUNEI
MALAYSIA
SINGAPORE

TANZANIA

PAPUA
NEW
GUINEA

INDONESIA

MALAWI

MADAGASCAR

MOZAMBIQUE

**MAJOR CHEMICAL ACCIDENTS/INCIDENTS
REPORTED** *1986-92*

more than 3 major chemical accidents/
incidents *number given*

3

2

1

other states

GUAM

WESTERN
SAMOA
FIJI

FRENCH
POLYNESIA

Queensland

AUSTRALIA

NEW
ZEALAND

New South
Wales

CANADA

UK
former USSR 10
MONGOLIA

U.S.A.
18
TURKEY
IRAN
CHINA
6

MEXICO
7
ALGERIA
LIBYA

SUDAN
6

ZAIRE

JAPAN

BRAZIL
INDONESIA

AUSTRALIA

Source: UN Environment Programme,
Environmental Data Report 1993-94.

CANADA

UNITED STATES
OF AMERICA
19.1%

UNITED
KINGDOM

DENMARK

EST
LAT
LITH

BELARUS

NETH

GERMANY

HUNGARY

POLAND

UKRAINE

FRANCE

ROMANIA

MOL

BEL

SPAIN

ITALY

former YUG

AUSTRIA

GREECE

BULG

GEO

TUR

TURKEY

AZER

IRAN

MEXICO

IRAQ

ALGERIA

EGYPT

COLOMBIA

VENEZUELA

SAUDI
ARABIA

ECUADOR

PERU

NIGERIA

BOLIVIA

BRAZIL

ZAIRE

ARGENTINA

SOUTH
AFRICA

average temperature
at beginning of 20th century

-1°C   1 million years ago

-2°C

-3°C

-4°C   previous ice ages

10,000 years ago

World temperatures are forecast to rise dramatically by 2100. Some islands will sink under the ocean and vast areas of land will be permanently inundated. Deserts and tropical diseases will spread.

GLOBAL WARMING:
STATES' SHARES OF
EMISSIONS OF MAIN
GREENHOUSE GASES
1991 top 50 emitters

states of 5% or over: percentage given

=1.0%
=0.1%
=0.01%

ENERGY EFFICIENCY:
KILOGRAMS OF OIL EQUIVALENT
USED PER U.S.100 DOLLARS OF
GROSS DOMESTIC PRODUCT (GDP)

1 kilogram = 2.2 lbs

48 kilograms
36
24

no data

Source: UNDP.

RUSSIA **8.7%**

CHINA **9.9%**

NORTH KOREA

SOUTH KOREA

JAPAN **5%**

STAN

KIRG

ISTAN

A

B-DESH

MYANMAR

THAILAND

VIETNAM

PHILIPPINES

MALAYSIA

I N D O N E S I A

AUSTRALIA

2090+ 5°C

+ 4°C

+ 3°C

+ 2°C

global warming?

medieval warm period

1990

+ 1°C

1900

years ago

little ice age

PAST AND FUTURE GLOBAL TEMPERATURES
COMPARED WITH AVERAGE TEMPERATURE
AT BEGINNING OF 20th CENTURY
degrees celsius

change in timescale

Source: IPCC.

CANADA

UNITED STATES
OF AMERICA
23.9%

IRELAND

UNITED
KINGDOM

DENMARK

NETH

BELGIUM

FRANCE

SWITZER

ITA

PORTUGAL

SPAIN

TUNISIA

ALGERIA

LIBYA

MOROCCO

EGY

GHANA

SUDAN

NIGERIA

ETHIOPI

CÔTE D'IVOIRE

KENYA

ZAIRE

TANZANIA

ZAMBIA

ZIMBABWE

SOUTH AFRICA

MEXICO

CUBA

TRINIDAD & TOBAGO

COLOMBIA

VENEZUELA

ECUADOR

PERU

CHILE

BRAZIL

ARGENTINA

TOP NET EXPORTERS OF ENERGY
1991 percentages
Source: United Nations.

Saudi Arabia 11.7%

former USSR 7.9%

Iran 4.9%

UAE 4.6%

Norway,
Venezuela 4.3%

Algeria,
Canada 3.3%

Nigeria 3.2%

Indonesia 3%

TOP NET IMPORTERS OF ENERGY
1991 percentages
Source: United Nations.

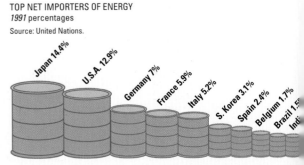

Japan 14.4%

U.S.A. 12.9%

Germany 7%

France 5.9%

Italy 5.2%

S. Korea 3.1%

Spain 2.4%

Belgium 1.7%

Brazil 1.5

Ind

The average person burns two and half times more energy in the U.S.A. than in Japan or Switzerland.

SWEDEN
FINLAND
ESTONIA
LATVIA
LITHUANIA
ERMANY
BELARUS
POLAND
UKRAINE
RUSSIA
9.4%
NORTH KOREA
IC
SLOVAKIA
A
HUNGARY
MOL
ROMANIA
CHINA
8.6%
JAPAN
5.1%
CRO
YUG
KAZAKHSTAN
SOUTH KOREA
B-H
BULGARIA
GREECE
GEO
UZBEKISTAN
TURKEY
AZER
TURK
KIRG
SYRIA
IRAN
ISRAEL
IRAQ
PAKISTAN
SAUDI ARABIA
UAE
NEPAL
BANGLADESH
MYAN
THAILAND
VIETNAM
INDIA
MALAYSIA
PHILIPPINES
SINGAPORE
INDONESIA
AUSTRALIA
NEW
ZEALAND

AVERAGE ENERGY USE PER HEAD
1991 gigajoules

260 gigajoules
200
150
100
50

no data

STATES' SHARES OF WORLD
ENERGY CONSUMPTION
1991 percentages of 80 states with
0.05% or more of world total

states of 5% or over: percentage given

= 1%

= 0.1%

Highest: UAE, 656 gigajoules; Canada, 328; U.S.A., 324
Lowest: Bangladesh, 4.4 gigajoules; Myanmar, 6.5; Vietnam, 7.7

Source: World Resources Institute, *World Resources 1994-95*.

UNITED STATES
OF AMERICA
31.1%

IRELAND

UNITED
KINGDOM

FRANCE

MEXICO

PORTUGAL   SPAIN

COLOMBIA   VENEZUELA

PERU

BRAZIL

URUGUAY

CHILE   ARGENTINA

TUNISIA

MOROCCO   LIBYA

ALGERIA   EGYPT

KENYA

NIGERIA

SOUTH
AFRICA

CONGESTION:
NUMBER OF VEHICLES PER KILOMETRE
OF PAVED ROAD *1992*
1 kilometre = 0.62 miles

Most congested: Bahrain, 701; Ecuador, 667; Hong Kong, 568

Sources: CIA; International Road Federation.

In 1992, there
were five times as
many vehicles per kilometre
of paved road as there
were in 1953.

France	Norway	Canada, UK	Germany, Thailand, U.S.A.	Belgium	Spain, Turkey	Colombia	Brazil
40	50	70	80	90	110	160	270

Michael Kidron and Ronald Segal *The State of the World Atlas* 5th edition   Copyright © Myriad Editions Limited

22

In 1950 there was one car for every 46 people in the world. In 1970 there was one for every 18; by 1994, one for every 12. Cars are running us down.

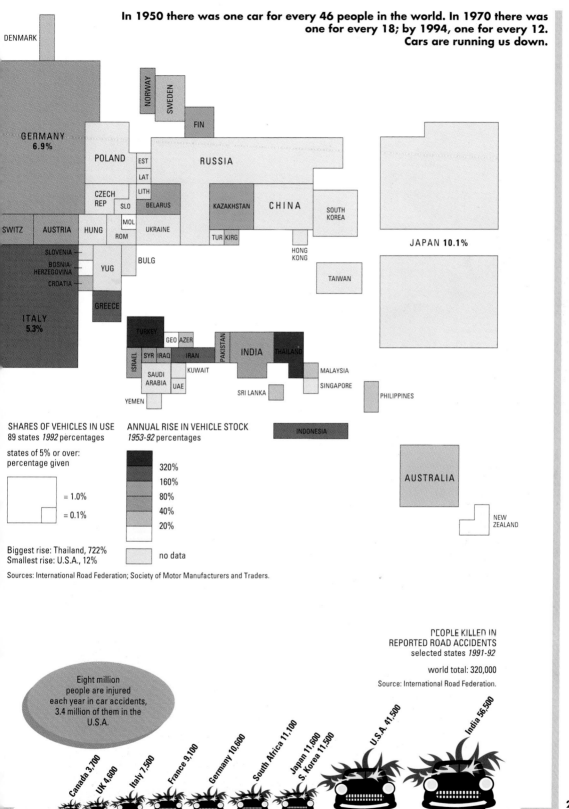

DENMARK

NORWAY

SWEDEN

FIN

GERMANY
6.9%

POLAND

EST

LAT

LITH

CZECH REP

SLO

BELARUS

RUSSIA

KAZAKHSTAN

CHINA

SOUTH KOREA

JAPAN 10.1%

SWITZ

AUSTRIA

HUNG

MOL

ROM

UKRAINE

TUR KIRG

HONG KONG

SLOVENIA

BOSNIA-HERZEGOVINA

CROATIA

YUG

BULG

TAIWAN

ITALY
5.3%

GREECE

TURKEY

GEO AZER

PAKISTAN

INDIA

THAILAND

ISRAEL

SYR IRAQ

IRAN

MALAYSIA

SINGAPORE

SAUDI ARABIA

UAE

KUWAIT

SRI LANKA

PHILIPPINES

YEMEN

INDONESIA

SHARES OF VEHICLES IN USE
89 states *1992* percentages

states of 5% or over:
percentage given

= 1.0%

= 0.1%

ANNUAL RISE IN VEHICLE STOCK
1953-92 percentages

- 320%
- 160%
- 80%
- 40%
- 20%

no data

Biggest rise: Thailand, 722%
Smallest rise: U.S.A., 12%

AUSTRALIA

NEW ZEALAND

Sources: International Road Federation; Society of Motor Manufacturers and Traders.

PEOPLE KILLED IN REPORTED ROAD ACCIDENTS
selected states *1991-92*

world total: 320,000

Source: International Road Federation.

Eight million people are injured each year in car accidents, 3.4 million of them in the U.S.A.

Canada 3,700

UK 4,600

Italy 7,500

France 9,100

Germany 10,600

South Africa 11,100

Japan 11,600
S. Korea 11,500

U.S.A. 41,500

India 56,500

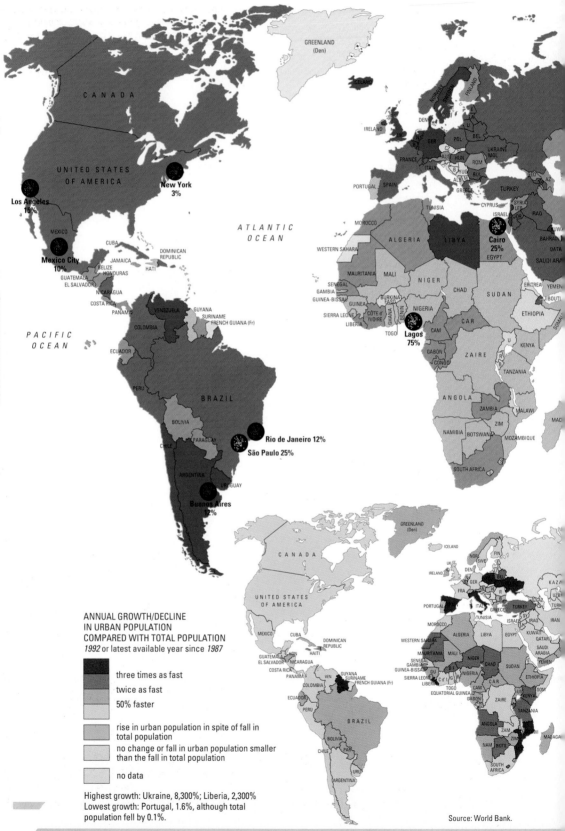

GREENLAND
(Den)

ICELAND

C A N A D A

UNITED STATES
OF AMERICA

New York
3%

Los Angeles
15%

MEXICO

Mexico City
10%

CUBA

DOMINICAN
REPUBLIC

JAMAICA
BELIZE
HONDURAS
GUATEMALA
EL SALVADOR
NICARAGUA
COSTA RICA
PANAMA

HAITI

ATLANTIC
OCEAN

PACIFIC
OCEAN

VENEZUELA

GUYANA
SURINAME
FRENCH GUIANA (Fr)

COLOMBIA

ECUADOR

PERU

B R A Z I L

BOLIVIA

PARAGUAY

CHILE

Rio de Janeiro 12%
São Paulo 25%

ARGENTINA

URUGUAY

Buenos Aires
12%

GREENLAND
(Den)

ICELAND

IRELAND

DEN

GER

POL

UKRAINE
MOL

FRANCE

ITALY

ROM

BUL

PORTUGAL   SPAIN

GREECE

TURKEY

CYPRUS

SYRIA
LEB

ISRAEL
JOR

IRAQ

KUW

MOROCCO

TUNISIA

AZ

ALGERIA

LIBYA

Cairo
25%

EGYPT

BAHRAIN

QATA

SAUDI AR

WESTERN SAHARA

MAURITANIA   MALI

NIGER

CHAD

SUDAN

ERITREA   YEMEN

DJIBOUTI

SENEGAL
GAMBIA
GUINEA-BISSAU
GUINEA
SIERRA LEONE

BURKINA
FASO

CÔTE d'
IVOIRE
GHANA

BENIN
NIGERIA

Lagos
75%

ETHIOPIA

LIBERIA

TOGO

CAM

CAR

U

SOM

KENYA

GABON
CONGO

ZAIRE

R

TANZANIA

A N G O L A

ZAMBIA

ZIM

MALAWI

MAD

NAMIBIA   BOTSWANA

MOZAMBIQUE

SOUTH AFRICA

ANNUAL GROWTH/DECLINE
IN URBAN POPULATION
COMPARED WITH TOTAL POPULATION
1992 or latest available year since *1987*

- three times as fast
- twice as fast
- 50% faster
- rise in urban population in spite of fall in total population
- no change or fall in urban population smaller than the fall in total population
- no data

Highest growth: Ukraine, 8,300%; Liberia, 2,300%
Lowest growth: Portugal, 1.6%, although total population fell by 0.1%.

GREENLAND
(Den)

ICELAND

UK
IRELAND

NOR
SWE
DEN
GER
FRA

FIN

KAZA

UZB
TURK

C A N A D A

UNITED STATES
OF AMERICA

PORTUGAL

ITALY
GREECE

TURKEY

SY
IRAQ

IRAN

MEXICO

CUBA

DOMINICAN
REPUBLIC

MOROCCO

TUNISIA

ISRAEL

EGYPT

KUWAIT

QATAR

SAUDI
ARABIA

GUATEMALA
EL SALVADOR   NICARAGUA
COSTA RICA
PANAMA

HAITI

WESTERN SAHARA

ALGERIA

LIBYA

YEMEN

VEN

GUYANA
SURINAME
FRENCH GUIANA (Fr)

GU

MAURITANIA   MALI
SENEGAL
GAMBIA
GUINEA-BISSAU

NIGER

CHAD

SUDAN

COLOMBIA

SIERRA LEONE
LIBERIA

NIGERIA

CAM

CAR

ETHIOPIA

ECUADOR

PERU

TOGO
EQUATORIAL GUINEA
GABON

UG
KENYA

ZAIRE

SOM

B R A Z I L

BOLIVIA

PAR

TANZANIA

ANGOLA

ZAM

ZIM

MALAWI

MADAGA

NAM   BOTS

CHILE

URU

SOUTH
AFRICA

ARGENTINA

Source: World Bank.

24

In all but a very few states, the urban population is growing faster than the total population. The consequences, from squalor to stress, are more evident than is the capacity to deal with them.

URBAN POPULATION
AS PROPORTION OF TOTAL POPULATION
1992 or latest available year since *1987* percentages

- 80%
- 60%
- 40%
- 20%

no data

Highest: Singapore, 100%; Bermuda, 99%
Lowest: Bhutan, Burundi, Rwanda, 6%

THE MEGACITIES:
POPULATION INCREASE *1990 to 2000*
percentage given

up to 25% increase

25% or over

Source: World Bank.

Beijing 32%
Tianjin 36%
Seoul 17%
Tokyo 12%
Osaka 1%
Shanghai 30%
Karachi 51%
Delhi 43%
Bombay 48%
Calcutta 19%
Dacca 74%
Manila 42%
Jakarta 46%

RUSSIA
 KAZAKHSTAN
MONGOLIA
KIRG
CHINA
N.KOREA
JAPAN
S KOREA
PAK
NEPAL
BHUTAN
INDIA
BDESH
MYANMAR
LAOS
VIETNAM
THAI
CAM
TAIWAN
PHILIPPINES
SRI LANKA
BRUNEI
MALAYSIA
INDONESIA
PAPUA NEW GUINEA
AUSTRALIA
NEW ZEALAND

THE MEGACITIES:
PROJECTED POPULATIONS OF THE WORLD'S 21 LARGEST CITIES
IN THE YEAR 2000

Source: World Resources Institute, *World Resources 1994-95*.

Cairo, Osaka 11m

Dacca, Delhi, Karachi, Rio de Janeiro 12m

Buenos Aires, Calcutta, Jakarta, Los Angeles, Manila, Seoul, Tianjin 13m

Beijing, Lagos 14m

Mexico City 16m

New York, Shanghai 17m

Bombay 18m

São Paulo 23m

Tokyo 28m

RUSSIA
MONGOLIA
N.KOREA
S KOREA
JAPAN
CHINA
TAIWAN
BDESH
MYAN
VIETNAM
THAI
PHILIPPINES
SRI LANKA
BRUNEI
MALAYSIA
INDONESIA
PAPUA NEW GUINEA
AUSTRALIA
NEW ZEALAND

People are not equal citizens within the world of states.
The average billionaire collects U.S. $200 million a year,
or as much as two million average Indians or Haitians or
six million average Ethiopians or Zaireans.

The top 101 private fortunes in the world, owned by 223
billionaire families, together claim income and capital
gains of U.S.$45.5 billion per year, the equivalent of 2.6
percent of world income.

Sources: *Fortune;* UN Development Programme.

223 billionaire families claim 2.6% of world income per year

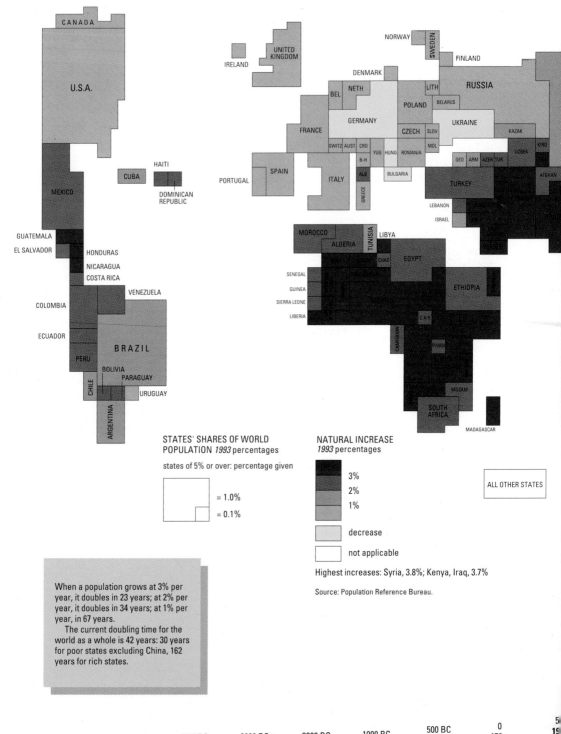

CANADA

U.S.A.

MEXICO

GUATEMALA
EL SALVADOR
HONDURAS
NICARAGUA
COSTA RICA

CUBA
HAITI
DOMINICAN
REPUBLIC

COLOMBIA

VENEZUELA

ECUADOR

PERU
BRAZIL
BOLIVIA
PARAGUAY
CHILE
URUGUAY
ARGENTINA

IRELAND
UNITED
KINGDOM

NORWAY
SWEDEN
FINLAND

DENMARK

BEL
NETH
GERMANY
FRANCE
SWITZ AUST CRO
B-H
PORTUGAL
SPAIN
ITALY
ALB
GREECE

POLAND
LITH
BELARUS
RUSSIA
CZECH SLOV
UKRAINE
KAZAK
YUG HUNG ROMANIA
MOL
BULGARIA
GEO ARM AZER TUR
UZBEK
KIRG
TURKEY
AFGHAN
LEBANON
ISRAEL

MOROCCO
TUNISIA
LIBYA
ALGERIA
CHAD
EGYPT
YEMEN

SENEGAL
GUINEA
SIERRA LEONE
LIBERIA
C A R
ETHIOPIA
CAMEROON
RWAN
MOZAM
SOUTH
AFRICA
MADAGASCAR

STATES' SHARES OF WORLD POPULATION *1993* percentages

states of 5% or over: percentage given

☐ = 1.0%
▫ = 0.1%

NATURAL INCREASE
1993 percentages

- 3%
- 2%
- 1%
- decrease
- not applicable

ALL OTHER STATES

Highest increases: Syria, 3.8%; Kenya, Iraq, 3.7%

Source: Population Reference Bureau.

When a population grows at 3% per year, it doubles in 23 years; at 2% per year, it doubles in 34 years; at 1% per year, in 67 years.
    The current doubling time for the world as a whole is 42 years: 30 years for poor states excluding China, 162 years for rich states.

10,000 BC
4m

5000 BC
5m

4000 BC
7m

3000 BC
14m

2000 BC
27m

1000 BC
50m

500 BC
100m

0
170m

5
19

There are 5,500 million people on earth and many more on the way.

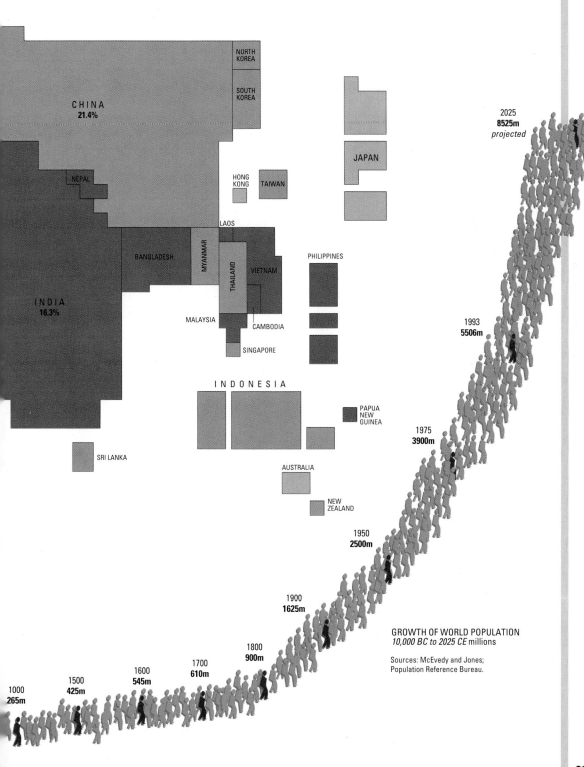

NORTH KOREA

SOUTH KOREA

CHINA
21.4%

JAPAN

NEPAL

HONG KONG

TAIWAN

LAOS

BANGLADESH

MYANMAR

THAILAND

VIETNAM

PHILIPPINES

INDIA
16.3%

MALAYSIA

CAMBODIA

SINGAPORE

INDONESIA

PAPUA NEW GUINEA

SRI LANKA

AUSTRALIA

NEW ZEALAND

2025
8525m
projected

1993
5506m

1975
3900m

1950
2500m

1900
1625m

1800
900m

1700
610m

1600
545m

1500
425m

1000
265m

GROWTH OF WORLD POPULATION
10,000 BC to 2025 CE millions

Sources: McEvedy and Jones;
Population Reference Bureau.

29

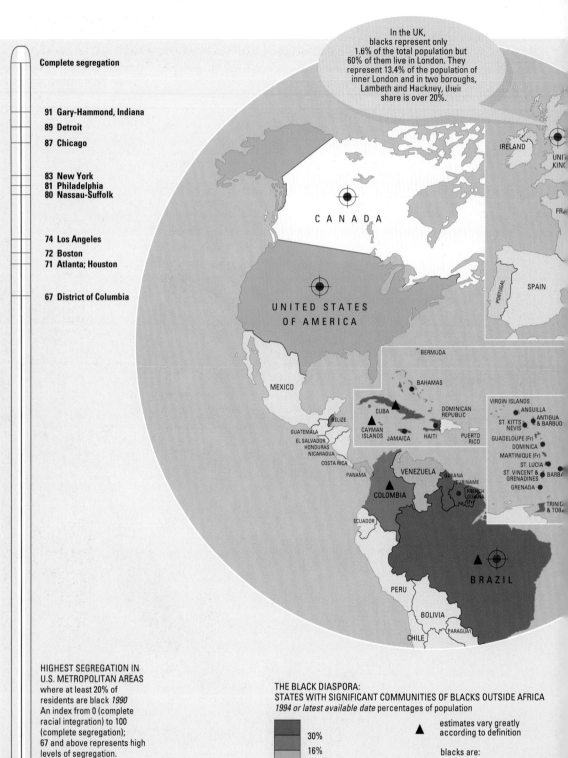

Complete segregation

91 Gary-Hammond, Indiana
89 Detroit
87 Chicago

83 New York
81 Philadelphia
80 Nassau-Suffolk

74 Los Angeles
72 Boston
71 Atlanta; Houston

67 District of Columbia

In the UK,
blacks represent only
1.6% of the total population but
60% of them live in London. They
represent 13.4% of the population of
inner London and in two boroughs,
Lambeth and Hackney, their
share is over 20%.

IRELAND
UNITED
KINGDOM
FRA
PORTUGAL
SPAIN

CANADA

UNITED STATES
OF AMERICA

BERMUDA

MEXICO
BAHAMAS
CUBA
DOMINICAN
REPUBLIC
BELIZE
CAYMAN
ISLANDS JAMAICA HAITI PUERTO
RICO
GUATEMALA
EL SALVADOR
HONDURAS
NICARAGUA
COSTA RICA
PANAMA

VENEZUELA GUYANA
SURINAME
COLOMBIA FRENCH
GUIANA
(Fr)

ECUADOR

BRAZIL

PERU

BOLIVIA
PARAGUAY
CHILE

VIRGIN ISLANDS
ANGUILLA
ANTIGUA
& BARBUD
ST. KITTS
NEVIS
GUADELOUPE (Fr)
DOMINICA
MARTINIQUE (Fr)
ST. LUCIA
ST. VINCENT &
GRENADINES BARBA
GRENADA
TRINIC
& TOBA

HIGHEST SEGREGATION IN
U.S. METROPOLITAN AREAS
where at least 20% of
residents are black *1990*
An index from 0 (complete
racial integration) to 100
(complete segregation);
67 and above represents high
levels of segregation.

Source: *USA Today.*

Complete integration

THE BLACK DIASPORA:
STATES WITH SIGNIFICANT COMMUNITIES OF BLACKS OUTSIDE AFRICA
1994 or latest available date percentages of population

30%
16%
11%
6%
1%

other states or no data

▲ estimates vary greatly
    according to definition

    blacks are:

⊕ a prime target of racism

• electorally dominant

Sources: Kurian; Minority Rights Group; Segal;
UK Census of Population; regional and national
handbooks and yearbooks.

Michael Kidron and Ronald Segal *The State of the World Atlas* 5th edition   Copyright © Myriad Editions .imited

Some diasporas prosper. Some do not. Either way, they are often the target of resentment and even violence.

Afghanistan
UK

Kenya
Lebanon
Libya
South Africa
Tanzania
Uganda
UAE
Zambia

Bangladesh
Bhutan

Canada
Grenada
Guyana
Guadeloupe
Jamaica
St Lucia
St Vincent
Suriname
Trinidad & Tobago
U.S.A.

Australia
Brunei
Fiji
Hong Kong
Malaysia
Mauritius
Myanmar
Nepal
Pakistan
Reunion
Singapore
Sri Lanka

THE INDIAN DIASPORA:
STATES WITH SIGNIFICANT COMMUNITIES OF INDIANS OUTSIDE INDIA
1994 or latest available date

Bangladesh   communities over 1 percent of population

Afghanistan   communities under 1 percent of population

Highest: Mauritius, 70% of total population; Guyana, 50%; Fiji, 48%;
Trinidad and Tobago, 41%

Sources: Kurian; Minority Rights Group; Parekh; UK Census of Population;
regional and national handbooks and yearbooks.

Italy
UK

Australia
Brunei
Cambodia
Indonesia
Philippines
Malaysia
Myanmar
Singapore
Taiwan
Thailand
Vietnam

Canada
Costa Rica
Paraguay
Jamaica
Suriname
Trinidad & Tobago
U.S.A.

THE CHINESE DIASPORA:
STATES WITH SIGNIFICANT COMMUNITIES OF OVERSEAS CHINESE
1994 or latest available date

Australia   communities over 0.5 percent of population

Afghanistan   communities under 0.5 percent of population

Highest: Singapore, 77% of total population; Malaysia, 30-35%; Brunei, 16%;
Thailand, 12%

Sources: *Independent*, London; Kurian; Minority Rights Group; UK Census of Population;
regional and national handbooks and yearbooks.

ICELAND

NORWAY   SWEDEN   FINLA

ESTON
LATVI
LITHUANIA
DENMARK

IRELAND   UNITED   NETH   POLAND   BELA
KINGDOM   BEL   UKRA
GERMANY   CZECH
REPUBLIC   SLOVAK
AUSTRIA   HUNGARY
FRANCE   SWITZ   SLO   ROMA
CROATIA
B - H   YUG
ITALY   ALB   BUL
PORTUGAL   M
SPAIN   GREECE

CANADA

UNITED STATES
OF AMERICA

BERMUDA

MEXICO   BAHAMAS

CUBA   DOMINICAN   VIRGIN
REPUBLIC   ISLANDS

BELIZE   CAYMAN   ST. KITTS NEVIS   ANTIGUA
GUATEMALA   ISLANDS   JAMAICA   HAITI   PUERTO   ANGUILLA   & BARBUDA
EL SALVADOR   RICO   GUADELOUPE
HONDURAS   DOMINICA
NICARAGUA   MARTINIQUE
COSTA RICA   ST. LUCIA
PANAMA   VENEZUELA   GUYANA   ST. VINCENT &   BARBADOS
SURINAME   GRENADINES
COLOMBIA   FRENCH   GRENADA
GUIANA   TRINIDAD
& TOBAGO

PACIFIC
OCEAN

ECUADOR

PERU   BRAZIL

BOLIVIA

CHILE   PARAGUAY

MOROCCO   TUNISIA

ALGERIA   LIB

WESTERN SAHARA

MAURITANIA   MALI   NIGER

SENEGAL   BURKINA   C
GAMBIA   FASO
GUINEA-BISSAU   GUINEA   NIGERIA
SIERRA LEONE   CÔTE d'
IVOIRE   GHANA   BENIN
LIBERIA   TOGO   CAMEROON
EQUATORIAL GUINEA   C

GABON
CONGO

ANGO

NAMIBI

URUGUAY

ARGENTINA

There are 20
states in which less
than half the population has
access to Western-style health
care. Seventeen of these
are in Africa.

AVERAGE LIFE EXPECTANCY AT BIRTH
1992 years

- 75 years
- 65
- 55
- 45

no data

Longest life expectancy: Japan, 79 years
Shortest life expectancy: Sierra Leone, 42 years

states claiming that 100% of their
population has access to Western-style
health care *1985-89*

Source: UNDP.

People live longer when they have access to health care and clean water.

PACIFIC OCEAN

SHARE OF POPULATION
WITH ACCESS TO SAFE DRINKING WATER
1988-91

all
two-thirds
one third

no data

Lowest: Uganda, 15%;
Congo, 21%; Ethiopia, 28%

Source: UNDP.

33

GREENLAND
(Den)

ICELAND

CANADA

UNITED STATES
OF AMERICA

NORWAY

SWEDEN

DENMARK

IRELAND UNITED
KINGDOM

NETH
BELY GERMANY CZECH
POLA

FRANCE AUS
ITALY R

62 Hungary

PORTUGAL SPAIN

53 Finland

MEXICO

BAHAMAS

ATLANTIC
OCEAN

MOROCCO

TUNISIA

ALGERIA

LIE

WESTERN SAHARA

CUBA

DOMINICAN
REPUBLIC

BELIZE JAMAICA HAITI
GUATEMALA HONDURAS
EL SALVADOR
NICARAGUA

COSTA RICA
PANAMA

BARBADOS

TRINIDAD & TOBAGO

VENEZUELA
GUYANA
SURINAME
FRENCH GUIANA (Fr)

MAURITANIA

MALI

NIGER

SENEGAL

GAM

GUINEA-BISSAU

GUINEA

SIERRA LEONE
LIBERIA

CÔTE d'
IVOIRE

BURKINA
FASO

GHANA

BENIN

TOGO

NIGERIA

CAMEROON

EQUATORIAL GUINEA

44 Russia

PACIFIC
OCEAN

COLOMBIA

ECUADOR

GABON

CONGO

37 Austria

35 Switzerland
34 Belgium

32 U.S.A.
31 Czech Republic, Denmark, France

29 Germany, Sweden

27 Bulgaria, Luxembourg, Poland
26 New Zealand
25 Norway
24 Australia
23 Canada, Iceland
22 Japan

ANG

NAMIE

PERU

BRAZIL

BOLIVIA

PARAGUAY

CHILE

URUGUAY

ARGENTINA

THE BEST IS INADEQUATE:
RELATIVE HUMAN DEVELOPMENT
1992 index

The Human Development Index
is based on three key components:
longevity, education, and income.

900	high
800	medium to high
700	medium
500	medium to low
300	low
	very low
	no data

17 Portugal

15 Ireland
14 Italy, Spain, UK
13 Netherlands
12 Israel

7 Greece, Malta

MURDER AND SUICIDE
BY MEN *1990* OECD states
per 100,000 people

OECD average: 26

Top: Canada, 932; Switzerland, 931; Japan, 929
Bottom: Guinea, 191; Burkina Faso, 203; Afghanistan, 208

Source: UNDP.

Most: Hungary, 62
Least: Greece, Malta, 7

Source: UNDP.

THE QUALITY OF LIFE 10

In life, quality and quantity mostly march in step.

YEARS OF LIFE LOST PREMATURELY
1990 per 1,000 people

world average: 35 years

125 years
100
75
50
25

no data

Source: UNDP.

35

GREENLAND
(Den)

ICELAND

CANADA

UNITED STATES
OF AMERICA

DENMARK
IRELAND   UNITED
KINGDOM
NETH.
POLA
GERMANY
CZECH
FRANCE   AUS
ITALY   B-H

MEXICO

CUBA
DOMINICAN
REPUBLIC
BELIZE   JAMAICA   HAITI
GUATEMALA   HONDURAS
EL SALVADOR
NICARAGUA
COSTA RICA
PANAMA

ATLANTIC
OCEAN

PORTUGAL   SPAIN

MOROCCO

WESTERN SAHARA

MAURITANIA

TUNISIA

ALGERIA

LIB

MALI

NIGER

SENEGAL
GAMBIA
GUINEA-BISSAU
GUINEA
SIERRA LEONE
LIBERIA

BURKINA
FASO
CÔTE d'
IVOIRE   GHANA   BENIN   NIGERIA
TOGO

CAMEROON

EQUATORIAL GUINEA

GABON
CONGO

ANGO

NAMIB

VENEZUELA   GUYANA
SURINAME
FRENCH GUIANA (Fr)
TRINIDAD & TOBAGO

COLOMBIA

ECUADOR

PACIFIC
OCEAN

BRAZIL

PERU

BOLIVIA

CHILE   PARAGUAY

URUGUAY

ARGENTINA

INCOMES:
AVERAGE REAL
PURCHASING POWER
PER PERSON PER YEAR *1990*
international dollars

The international dollar is a measure
which attempts to gauge what states
could buy if they all shopped in a single
world supermarket.

- $16,000
- $8,000
- $4,000
- $2,000
- $1,000

no data

Highest: U.S.A., $21,449
Lowest: Ethiopia, $369

Sources: UNDP; World Bank.

INEQUALITY:
DIFFERENCE IN INCOME BETWEEN THE RICHEST
10 PERCENT AND THE POOREST 20 PERCENT *1990*
selected states

Sources: UNDP; World Bank.

5 to 10 times

3 to 5 times

Canada, China,
Denmark, Ethiopia,
Finland, France,
Germany, Ghana, India,
Israel, Italy, Netherlands,
Norway, Pakistan,
Spain, Sweden,
Uganda, UK

Australia, Colombia,
Costa Rica, Hong Kong
Lesotho, Malaysia,
Mexico, New Zealand
Peru, Singapore,
Switzerland,
Thailand, U.S.A.,
Venezuela

The poor may inherit the earth some day. Meanwhile the rich are in possession.

RUSSIA

KAZAKHSTAN

MONGOLIA

N KOREA

JAPAN

S KOREA

GEO

AZER

UZBEKISTAN

KIRGISTAN

TURKMEN

TAJ

CHINA

PACIFIC
OCEAN

URKEY

SYRIA

LEB

IRAQ

IRAN

AFGHANISTAN

EL

JOR

KUWAIT

BAHRAIN

QATAR UAE

PAKISTAN

BHUTAN

NEPAL

TAIWAN

SAUDI ARABIA

OMAN

B
DESH

INDIA

MYANMAR

LAOS

HONG KONG

ERITREA

YEMEN

DJIBOUTI

VIETNAM

THAILAND

AN

CAM

PHILIPPINES

ETHIOPIA

SOMALIA

SRI LANKA

BRUNEI

JGANDA

KENYA

MALAYSIA

SINGAPORE

TANZANIA

SEYCHELLES

COMOROS

INDONESIA

PAPUA
NEW
GUINEA

SOLOMON
ISLANDS

MALAWI

MADAGASCAR

MAURITIUS

MOZAMBIQUE

WESTERN SAMOA

AUSTRALIA

FIJI

over 20 times

10 to 20 times

NEW
ZEALAND

**Chile, Honduras,
Kenya, Tanzania**

**Botswana, Brazil,
Guatemala, Panama**

GREENLAND
(Den)

ICELAND

CANADA

UNITED STATES
OF AMERICA

1.3 billion
people live in
absolute poverty. 600 million
suffer from chronic
malnutrition.

MEXICO

CUBA
BELIZE   DOMINICAN
JAMAICA   REPUBLIC
HONDURAS   HAITI
GUATEMALA
EL SALVADOR
NICARAGUA
COSTA RICA
PANAMA

ATLANTIC
OCEAN

PACIFIC
OCEAN

VENEZUELA
GUYANA
SURINAME
FRENCH GUIANA (Fr)
TRINIDAD & TOBAGO

COLOMBIA

ECUADOR

BRAZIL

PERU

BOLIVIA

PARAGUAY

CHILE

URUGUAY

ARGENTINA

NORWAY
SWEDEN
DENMARK
IRELAND
UNITED
KINGDOM
NETH
BEL
GERMANY
POLA
CZECH
AUS
FRANCE
ITALY
PORTUGAL   SPAIN
TUNISIA
MOROCCO
ALGERIA
LIB
WESTERN SAHARA
MAURITANIA
MALI
NIGER
SENEGAL
GAMBIA
BURKINA
FASO
GUINEA-BISSAU
GUINEA
BENIN
GHANA
NIGERIA
SIERRA LEONE
CÔTE d'
IVOIRE
LIBERIA
TOGO
CAMEROON
EQUATORIAL GUINEA
GABON
CONGO
ANGC
NAMIB

FEAST AND FAMINE:
AVERAGE CALORIES AVAILABLE
AS A PROPORTION OF NEED
1994-95 percentages

- 120%
- 110%
- 100%
- 90%
- 80%

no data

Highest: Ireland, 157%; Belgium, 149%
Lowest: Ethiopia, Chad, 73%; Mozambique, 77%

Sources: UN; World Resources Institute,
World Resources 1994-95.

STUNTED CHILDREN
AS A PROPORTION OF CHILD POPULAT
AGED 2 TO 5 YEARS *1980-91*

- 50%
- 25%
- 10%

no data

Highest: Guatemala, 68%; Bangladesh,
Mauritania, 65%
Lowest: Trinidad and Tobago, 4%; Jama
Venezuela, 7%

40 million people die each year from hunger-related diseases - the equivalent of over 300 jumbo-jet crashes a day with no survivors. Half the passengers are children.

RUSSIA

KAZAKHSTAN

MONGOLIA

N.KOREA   JAPAN

S.KOREA

GEO   UZBEKISTAN   KIRGISTAN

AZER   TURKMEN   TAJ

TURKEY   CHINA

SYRIA   IRAQ   IRAN   AFGHANISTAN

DEB   KUWAIT   PAKISTAN   NEPAL   BHUTAN

JOR   BAHRAIN   B.DESH

QATAR   UAE

SAUDI ARABIA   OMAN   INDIA   MYANMAR   LAOS

THAILAND   VIETNAM

ERITREA   YEMEN   CAM   PHILIPPINES

DJIBOUTI

ETHIOPIA   SOMALIA   SRI LANKA   BRUNEI

UGANDA   KENYA   MALAYSIA

TANZANIA   SINGAPORE

INDONESIA   PAPUA NEW GUINEA

MALAWI   MADAGASCAR

MAURITIUS

MOZAMBIQUE

PACIFIC OCEAN

AUSTRALIA

NEW ZEALAND

CANADA

UNITED STATES OF AMERICA   RUSSIA   KAZAKHSTAN   MONGOLIA   JAPAN

TURKEY   IRAN   CHINA

ALGERIA   LIBYA   INDIA

SUDAN

BRAZIL   ZAIRE

INDONESIA

AUSTRALIA

Sources: UN; World Resources Institute, *World Resources 1994-95*.

39

INTERNATIONAL TELECOMMUNICATIONS
TRAFFIC OF INDIVIDUAL STATES COMPARED
WITH THAT OF THE U.S.A. *1992*
43 states (and U.S.A.) at least 44 millions MiTTs
(minutes of international telecoms traffic)

In 1992:
U.S.A.: 9,820 million MiTTs
Iceland: 44 million MiTTs

Source: Telegeography.

50% - 75% of U.S. tra
France
UK

over 75% of U.S. traffic
Germany

U.S.A. 100%

GREENLAND
(Den)

U.S.A.
Sweden
ICELAND

Sweden

Sweden

U.S.A.

C A N A D A

NORWAY
SWEDEN
FINLAND

UNITED
KINGDOM

IRELAND
DEN
Germany
N
POL
BEL
B
GER
CZ
UKRAINE
A
HUN
UK
FRANCE
ROM
Germany
SPAIN
B Y
BULG
Germany
GREECE
TURKEY
G
AZE
A
PORTUGAL
Germany

UNITED STATES
OF AMERICA

U.S.A.

MEXICO
CUBA

DOMINICAN
REPUBLIC
HATI
BELIZE
HONDURAS
GUATEMALA
EL SALVADOR
NICARAGUA
COSTA RICA
PANAMA
VENEZUELA
GUYANA
SURINAME
FRENCH GUIANA (Fr)
U.S.A.
COLOMBIA
ECUADOR
PERU
U.S.A.
U.S.A.
B R A Z I L
BOLIVIA
CHILE
PAR
URU
ARGENTINA
Argentina

PORTUGAL

TUNISIA
MOROCCO
ISRAEL
IRAQ
SYR
J
KUWAIT
WESTERN SAHARA
ALGERIA
LIBYA
EGYPT
QATA
SAUDI
ARAB
MAURITANIA
MALI
NIGER
CHAD
SUDAN
E
YEM
SENEGAL
GAMBIA
GUINEA-BISSAU
GUINEA
B F
B
NIGERIA
SIERRA LEONE
CÔTE d
G
IVOIRE
LIBERIA
TOGO
CAM
C A R
ETHIOPIA
EQUATORIAL GUINEA
UG
KENYA
GABON
ZAIRE
CON
TANZANIA
ANGOLA
ZAMBIA
MALAWI
ZIM
MADAGASCA
NAMIBIA
BOTS
MOZAMBIQUE
SOUTH
AFRICA

40

Some people see the world as their village. Most see their village as the world. They keep in contact with people they consider to be their neighbours.

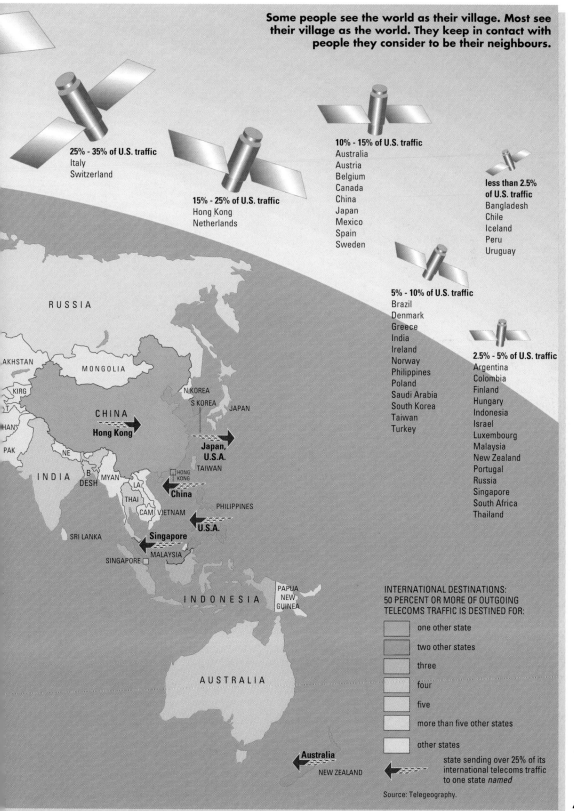

25% - 35% of U.S. traffic
Italy
Switzerland

15% - 25% of U.S. traffic
Hong Kong
Netherlands

10% - 15% of U.S. traffic
Australia
Austria
Belgium
Canada
China
Japan
Mexico
Spain
Sweden

less than 2.5% of U.S. traffic
Bangladesh
Chile
Iceland
Peru
Uruguay

5% - 10% of U.S. traffic
Brazil
Denmark
Greece
India
Ireland
Norway
Philippines
Poland
Saudi Arabia
South Korea
Taiwan
Turkey

2.5% - 5% of U.S. traffic
Argentina
Colombia
Finland
Hungary
Indonesia
Israel
Luxembourg
Malaysia
New Zealand
Portugal
Russia
Singapore
South Africa
Thailand

RUSSIA

AKHSTAN

MONGOLIA

KIRG

N.KOREA
S KOREA
JAPAN

CHINA
Hong Kong

HANS

PAK

NE

**Japan,
U.S.A.**

TAIWAN

INDIA

B
DESH

MYAN

HONG
KONG

China

LA

THAI

CAM

VIETNAM

PHILIPPINES

U.S.A.

SRI LANKA

Singapore

SINGAPORE

MALAYSIA

INDONESIA

PAPUA
NEW
GUINEA

INTERNATIONAL DESTINATIONS:
50 PERCENT OR MORE OF OUTGOING
TELECOMS TRAFFIC IS DESTINED FOR:

one other state

two other states

three

four

five

more than five other states

other states

AUSTRALIA

Australia

NEW ZEALAND

state sending over 25% of its
international telecoms traffic
to one state *named*

Source: Telegeography.

ICELAND

NORWAY
SWEDEN
FINLAN

ESTONIA
LATVIA
DENMARK
LITHUANIA

IRELAND
UNITED
KINGDOM
NETH
BEL
GERMANY
CZECH
REPUBLIC
POLAND
BELA
UKRA
SLOVAK
FRANCE
SWITZ
AUSTRIA
HUNGARY
SLO
CROATIA
ROMAN
B - H
YUG
B
ITALY
ALB
M
GREECE

PORTUGAL
SPAIN

C A N A D A

UNITED STATES
OF AMERICA

ATLANTIC
OCEAN

MOROCCO
TUNISIA

WESTERN SAHARA
ALGERIA
LIB

MEXICO
HAITI
DOMINICAN
REPUBLIC
CUBA
BELIZE
JAMAICA
ST KITTS NEVIS
GUATEMALA
HONDURAS
EL SALVADOR
NICARAGUA
GRENADA
BARBADOS
COSTA RICA
TRINIDAD & TOBAGO
PANAMA
VENEZUELA
GUYANA
COLOMBIA
SURINAME
FRENCH GUIANA (Fr)

CAPE VERDE
MAURITANIA
MALI
NIGER
CH
SENEGAL
GAMBIA
GUINEA-BISSAU
BURKINA
FASO
BENIN
NIGERIA
GUINEA
SIERRA LEONE
CÔTE d'
IVOIRE
GHANA
TOGO
CA
LIBERIA
CAMEROON
GABON
CONGO
Z
SAO TOME
& PRINCIPE
EQUATORIAL
GUINEA
ANGO

PACIFIC
OCEAN

ECUADOR

PERU

B R A Z I L

NAMIBIA

ILLITERACY
AMONGST THOSE OF 15 YEARS AND OLDER
1990 or latest available date
percentages

BOLIVIA

PARAGUAY
CHILE

URUGUAY
ARGENTINA

70%
50%
30%
10%

no data

Highest: Bhutan, 85%; Sierra Leone, 79%; Guinea, 76%

illiteracy of women over 50%
higher than illiteracy of men

illiteracy of men higher than
illiteracy of women

Seventy-one percent of women in Peru are
illiterate - nearly nine times as many as the
proportion of men.

Sources: CIA; *Europa Regional Yearbook 1993, 1994;*
Social Indicators of Development; World Bank.

In most states, many people never learn to read or write. Educational neglect or other discrimination ensures that in all but a very few, more women than men are illiterate.

GREENLAND
(Den)

ICELAND

CANADA

NORWAY

SWEDEN

DENMARK

IRELAND

UNITED
KINGDOM

NETH.
BEL.
GERMANY

POLAN

CZECH

FRANCE

AUS

HU

ITALY

B-H

PORTUGAL   SPAIN

UNITED STATES
OF AMERICA

MEXICO

BAHAMAS

ATLANTIC
OCEAN

MOROCCO

ALGERIA

LIB

TUNISIA

WESTERN SAHARA

CUBA

DOMINICAN
REPUBLIC

BELIZE   JAMAICA
HAITI

ANTIGUA

CAPE VERDE

MAURITANIA

MALI

NIGER

GUATEMALA
EL SALVADOR
HONDURAS

SENEGAL
GAMBIA

CH

NICARAGUA

BARBADOS

GUINEA-BISSAU

BURKINA
FASO

BENIN

NIGERIA

COSTA RICA
PANAMA

TRINIDAD & TOBAGO

VENEZUELA

GUYANA

GUINEA

SIERRA LEONE

CÔTE d'
IVOIRE

GHANA

PACIFIC
OCEAN

COLOMBIA

SURINAME
FRENCH GUIANA (Fr)

LIBERIA

TOGO

CAMEROON

C

ECUADOR

EQUATORIAL GUINEA

GABON

BRAZIL

CONGO

Z

PERU

ANGO

BOLIVIA

NAMIBIA

PARAGUAY

CHILE

URUGUAY

ARGENTINA

DEATHS OF CHILDREN
UNDER FIVE-YEARS-OLD
per 1,000 live births
1992 or latest available date

- 200 (1 in 5)
- 100
- 50
- 30
- 10 (1 in 100)

- no data

Lowest: Japan, 6: Ireland, Singapore, 7
Highest: Mozambique, 276; Afghanistan, 243

more than 1 in 10 infants
die before their first birthday

Lowest: Iceland, Japan, 1 in 200
Highest: Afghanistan, Mali, 1 in 6

Sources: World Bank, *Social Indicators of Development 1994*;
World Resources Institute, *World Resources 1994-95*.

44

MISSING OUT:
CHILDREN NOT IN SECONDARY EDUCATION
1992 or latest available date
percentage of relevant age group

- 75%
- 50%
- 25%
- 10%

In 13 states,
including 11 in Africa, over
90% of children of secondary
school age are not in
secondary education.

- no data

Source: World Bank, *Social Indicators of
Development 1994*.

Poverty wastes lives. Children in poor states are less likely to survive, and less likely to get an adequate schooling.

GREENLAND
(Den)

ICELAND

NORWAY

SWEDEN

DENMARK

IRELAND

UNITED
KINGDOM

NETH

POLAN

BEL GERMANY CZECH

C A N A D A

FRANCE

AUS HU

S

B-H

ITALY

PORTUGAL   SPAIN

UNITED STATES
OF AMERICA

MOROCCO

TUNISIA

ALGERIA

LIB

WESTERN SAHARA

MEXICO

CUBA

DOMINICAN
REPUBLIC

A T L A N T I C
O C E A N

MAURITANIA

MALI

NIGER

BELIZE   JAMAICA   HAITI

GUATEMALA   HONDURAS

SENEGAL

CH

EL SALVADOR

GAMBIA

BURKINA
FASO

GUINEA-BISSAU

NICARAGUA

GUINEA

NIGERIA

COSTA RICA

TRINIDAD & TOBAGO

SIERRA LEONE

CÔTE d'
IVOIRE

GHANA

BENIN

PANAMA

VENEZUELA

GUYANA

LIBERIA

CAMEROON

SURINAME

TOGO

FRENCH GUIANA (Fr)

EQUATORIAL GUINEA

COLOMBIA

P A C I F I C
O C E A N

GABON

ECUADOR

CONGO

ANGO

B R A Z I L

DEFICIT IN THE NUMBER OF WOMEN
AS A RESULT OF DISCRIMINATION
early 1990s percentages

PERU

Actual number of women compared with the
number that might have lived had they enjoyed
the same treatment they get in states of high
human development (for example, Canada,
Japan, Norway, Sweden, Switzerland).

BOLIVIA

NAMIBI

PARAGUAY

CHILE

10% deficit

5%

2.5%

URUGUAY

ARGENTINA

surplus of women: in some cases
perhaps caused by war and/or homicide

least discriminating states:
number of women is 97% the number of men

no data

deficit of more than 500,000 women

Sources: UN; U.S. State Department.

If women worldwide enjoyed the same treatment as they do in Canada, Japan, Norway, Sweden and Switzerland, there would be 120 million more women alive. If they enjoyed fully-equal treatment with men, there would be many tens of millions more.

In 1992, there were 20 million fewer women than men in China.

RATIO OF WOMEN TO MEN STUDENTS IN HIGHER (INCLUDING VOCATIONAL) EDUCATION *early 1990s or latest available data*

- 25 women to every 100 men
- 50
- more women than men
- no data

Source: UNESCO.

ICELAND

NORWAY

SWEDEN

FINLAN

ESTONI

LATVI

LITHUANIA

DENMARK

IRELAND

UNITED
KINGDOM

NETH

BEL

L

GERMANY

POLAND

BELA

UKRA

CZECH
REPUBLIC

SLOVAK

FRANCE

SWITZ

AUSTRIA

HUNGARY

ROMAN

SLO

CROATIA

ITALY

B - H

YUG

BULG

PORTUGAL

SPAIN

ALB

M

GREECE

CANADA

UNITED STATES
OF AMERICA

MEXICO

ATLANTIC
OCEAN

MOROCCO

TUNISIA

WESTERN SAHARA

ALGERIA

CUBA

DOMINICAN
REPUBLIC

BELIZE

JAMAICA

GUATEMALA

HONDURAS

HAITI

SENE

EL SALVADOR

GAMBIA

GUINEA-BISSAU

NICARAGUA

COSTA RICA

VENEZUELA

TRINIDAD & TOBAGO

GUINEA

PANAMA

GUYANA

SIERRA LEONE

GHANA

NIGERIA

PACIFIC
OCEAN

SURINAME

FRENCH GUIANA (Fr)

LIBERIA

COLOMBIA

EQUATORIAL
GUINEA

CAMEROON

ECUADOR

TOGO

CONGO

PERU

BRAZIL

BOLIVIA

A WOMAN'S RIGHT TO CHOOSE?
LEGALLY AVAILABLE ABORTION
1993

ANGO

NAMIBI

CHILE

PARAGUAY

on request

for economic and medical reasons

if health of the women or child is at risk,
and in cases of rape or incest

URUGUAY

to save the woman's life,
and in cases of rape or incest

ARGENTINA

to save the woman's life

no data

ACCESS TO BIRTH CONTROL
1992 where known

poor

very poor

Sources: Population Action International; PCC.

Authority everywhere tries to stamp itself on women's bodies.

BEHIND CLOSED DOORS:
WIFE-BEATING AND MARITAL RAPE
early 1990s

reported as widespread

reported as significant

reported as rare

no data

Sources: U.S. Department of State; authors' judgement.

ICELAND

NORWAY SWEDEN FINLA

ESTO

DENMARK LATV

LITHUANIA

IRELAND UNITED KINGDOM BEL

NETH POLAND UKR

BEL GERMANY

FRANCE CZECH REPUBLIC SLOVAK

AUSTRIA HUNGARY

SWITZ SLO ROMAN

CROATIA

B - H YUG BULG

PORTUGAL SPAIN ITALY ALB M

GREECE

CANADA

UNITED STATES
OF AMERICA

*ATLANTIC
OCEAN*

MOROCCO TUNISIA

ALGERIA LIB

WESTERN SAHARA

BAHAMAS

MEXICO CUBA HAITI DOMINICAN REPUBLIC

CAPE VERDE MAURITANIA MALI NIGER

JAMAICA

BELIZE SENEGAL

GUATEMALA HONDURAS GAMBIA BURKINA FASO NIGERIA

EL SALVADOR GUINEA- GUINEA

NICARAGUA BISSAU BENIN

COSTA RICA GRENADA SIERRA LEONE CÔTE d' GHANA

PANAMA TRINIDAD & TOBAGO LIBERIA IVOIRE

VENEZUELA GUYANA TOGO EQUATORIAL CAMEROON

SURINAME GUINEA GABON

COLOMBIA FRENCH GUIANA (Fr) SAO TOME CONGO

& PRINCIPE

ECUADOR

9.8 U.S.A.

BRAZIL ANGO

PERU NAMI

8.1 Denmark

BOLIVIA

7.4 Japan

6.9 New Zealand

6.2 Finland

5.7 Hungary
5.5 Australia CHILE PARAGUAY

4.9 Switzerland
4.7 Bulgaria URUGUAY

4.3 Austria, Belgium ARGENTINA

3.9 U.K.

3.5 Germany CHILD LABOUR:
MINIMUM AGE OF LEGAL EMPLOYMENT
3.1 France *1993*

2.7 Canada

2.4 Poland 12 years or no legal minimum

2.1 Netherlands

1.7 Norway 13 years

14 years

INFANT DEATHS 15 years

FROM PRESUMED ABUSE

0.9 Sweden per 100,000 live births *1994* 16 years or over

selected countries

0.4 Italy no data

0.2 Spain

Source: UNICEF. minimum age limit rarely enforced,
especially in agriculture and informal
economy

Sources: International Confederation of Free Trade
Unions; U.S. State Department.

Children are widely exploited, not least for their labour.

RUSSIA

KAZAKHSTAN

MONGOLIA

NE

GEO

AZER

URKEY

TURKMEN

UZBEKISTAN

KIRGISTAN

TAJ.

N KOREA

JAPAN

S KOREA

SYRIA

LEB

EL

JOR

IRAQ

KUWAIT

IRAN

AFGHANISTAN

PAKISTAN

CHINA

TAIWAN

BAHRAIN

QATAR

UAE

OMAN

SAUDI ARABIA

NEPAL

BHUTAN

B'DESH

HONG KONG

ERITREA

YEMEN

DJIBOUTI

INDIA

MYANMAR

LAOS

VIETNAM

THAI

CAM

PACIFIC OCEAN

N

ETHIOPIA

SOMALIA

MALDIVES

SRI LANKA

PHILIPPINES

KIRIBATI

UGANDA

KENYA

BRUNEI

MALAYSIA

SINGAPORE

TANZANIA

COMOROS

INDONESIA

PAPUA NEW GUINEA

SOLOMON ISLANDS

MALAWI

MADAGASCAR

MAURITIUS

MOZAMBIQUE

WESTERN SAMOA

AUSTRALIA

FIJI

NEW ZEALAND

REPORTED SEXUAL ABUSE OF CHILDREN BY FOREIGN BUSINESSMEN OR TOURISTS *1994*

Latin America	Africa	Asia
Argentina	Benin	Bangladesh
Brazil	Côte d'Ivoire	Cambodia
Chile	Guinea	India
Colombia	Kenya	Indonesia
Costa Rica	Mali	S Korea
Cuba	Mauritania	Pakistan
Dominican	Morocco	Philippines
Republic	Senegal	Sri Lanka
El Salvador	Zaire	Taiwan
Guatemala		Thailand
Haiti		Vietnam
Mexico		
Peru		
Uruguay		

Source: UNICEF.

NUMBER OF CHILD PROSTITUTES *1994*
India 300,000
Philippines, Taiwan, Thailand 100,000
Pakistan, Vietnam 40,000
Sri Lanka 30,000

Source: UNICEF.

Michael Kidron and Ronald Segal *The State of the World Atlas* 5th edition   Copyright © Myriad Editions Limited

GREENLAND
(Den)

ICELAND

NORWAY   SWEDEN

DENMARK

C
IRELAND   UNITED
            KINGDOM

NETH.   POLA
BEL.   GERMANY   CZECH
LUX.   AUS.   H
            FRANCE   R.
                    ITALY

CANADA

UNITED STATES
OF AMERICA

ATLANTIC
OCEAN

PORTUGAL   SPAIN

MAL

MEXICO

MOROCCO
                        TUNISIA

WESTERN SAHARA   ALGERIA   LIB

CUBA
            DOMINICAN
            REPUBLIC
JAMAICA
BELIZE   HAITI
HONDURAS
GUATEMALA
EL SALVADOR
NICARAGUA
COSTA RICA
PANAMA

MAURITANIA   MALI   NIGER

China 3 million

SENEGAL   C
GAMBIA
GUINEA-BISSAU   BURKINA
            GUINEA   FASO
SIERRA LEONE   CÔTE d'   BENIN   NIGERIA
            IVOIRE GHANA
LIBERIA   TOGO   CAMEROON

BARBADOS
TRINIDAD & TOBAGO

VENEZUELA
            GUYANA
            SURINAME
            FRENCH GUIANA (Fr)

PACIFIC
OCEAN

COLOMBIA

EQUATORIAL GUINEA
                    GABON
                    CONGO

ECUADOR

BRAZIL

ANG

PERU

BOLIVIA

NAMIB

CHILE   PARAGUAY

CHAINED SMOKERS:
AVERAGE DAILY CONSUMPTION OF
MANUFACTURED CIGARETTES
PER SMOKER *1993*

U.S.A. 600,000

URUGUAY

ARGENTINA

India 510,000

24
18
12
6
3

no data

Brazil 380,000

Turkey 250,000

Most: United Arab Emirates, 38; Malta, 36; Brunei, 33; Japan, 27;
Switzerland, 24; U.S.A., 22; Germany, 18; France, 15; UK, 13

Source: U.S. Department of Agriculture.

Zimbabwe 160,000

Indonesia 140,000

TOP PRODUCERS OF RAW TOBACCO
1994 tonnes dry weight

Source: U.S. Department of Agriculture.

52

Each day, between 1.3 and 1.4 billion people consume more than 17,000 tonnes of tobacco.

"One tonne of tobacco = one million cigarettes = one death"
Richard Peto, 1993

RUSSIA

KAZAKHSTAN

MONGOLIA

NE

GEO
AZER
URKEY   TURKMEN   UZBEKISTAN   KIRGISTAN

SYRIA   TAJ.
LEB
EL   JOR   IRAQ   AFGHANISTAN   CHINA
         IRAN
T

KUWAIT
BAHRAIN   PAKISTAN
QATAR
UAE
SAUDI ARABIA   NEPAL   BHUTAN
              OMAN   B
                                       DESH
AN   INDIA
   ERITREA   YEMEN
         DJIBOUTI   MYANMAR
                                                          LAOS
ETHIOPIA   THAILAND
                SOMALIA   CAM
JGANDA
   KENYA

N.KOREA
S KOREA   JAPAN

TAIWAN

HONG KONG

VIETNAM

PACIFIC
OCEAN

PHILIPPINES

SEYCHELLES

TANZANIA

MALAWI   MADAGASCAR

MAURITIUS

IOZAMBIQUE

SRI LANKA

BRUNEI
MALAYSIA

INDONESIA

PAPUA
NEW
GUINEA

SOLOMON
ISLANDS

AUSTRALIA

WESTERN SAMOA

FIJI

NEW
ZEALAND

Exporters		Importers	
Brazil 230,000			
U.S.A. 200,000		200,000 U.S.A.	
		180,000 Germany	
Zimbabwe 190,000		130,000 UK	
Turkey 130,000		125,000 Russia	
Greece 110,000		120,000 Japan	
Italy 100,000		90,000 Netherlands	
Malawi 100,000		50,000 Spain	

TOP TRADERS IN RAW TOBACCO
1994 tonnes dry weight

Source: U.S. Department of Agriculture.

AIDS
REPORTED RATES OF AIDS
PER 100,000 POPULATION
1992 or latest available data

- 50 per 100,000
- 25
- 15
- 5
- 1

no cases reported

no data

Highest rate per 100,000: Bahamas, 104;
Namibia, 103; Congo, 85

more than 10,000 AIDS cases
reported to March 1994 *numbers given*

Source: WHO.

HIV-RELATED DEATHS OF ADULTS

2m
by 1994

8m
by 2000

HIV-INFECTED ADULTS

13-14m
by 1994

20m
by 2000

Source: WHO.

Map labels:

ICELAND, NORWAY, SWEDEN, FINLAN, DENMARK, ESTON, LATVI, LITHUANIA, IRELAND, UNITED KINGDOM, NETH, BEL, POLAND, BELA, **11,179** GERMANY, CZECH REPUBLIC, SLOVAK, UKR, **30,003** FRANCE, SWITZ, AUSTRIA, HUNGARY, ROMA, SLO, CROATIA, B-H, YUG, M, **21,770** ITALY, ALB, BULG, PORTUGAL, **24,202** SPAIN, GREECE

CANADA, UNITED STATES OF AMERICA **411,907**, MEXICO **18,353**

BERMUDA, BAHAMAS, CUBA, DOMINICAN REPUBLIC, JAMAICA, HAITI, BELIZE, HONDURAS, GUATEMALA, EL SALVADOR, NICARAGUA, COSTA RICA, PANAMA, ANGUILLA, ANTIGUA & BARBUDA, ST KITTS NEVIS, GUADELOUPE, DOMINICA, MARTINIQUE, ST LUCIA, ST VINCENT & GRENADINES, BARBADOS, GRENADA, TRINIDAD & TOBAGO, NETHERLANDS ANTILLES

ATLANTIC OCEAN, PACIFIC OCEAN

VENEZUELA, GUYANA, SURINAME, FRENCH GUIANA (Fr), COLOMBIA, ECUADOR, PERU, BRAZIL **49,312**, BOLIVIA, PARAGUAY, CHILE, URUGUAY, ARGENTINA

MOROCCO, TUNISIA, ALGERIA, LIB, WESTERN SAHARA, MAURITANIA, MALI, NIGER, CAPE VERDE, SENEGAL, GAMBIA, GUINEA-BISSAU, GUINEA, BURKINA FASO, BENIN, NIGERIA, SIERRA LEONE, CÔTE d'IVOIRE, GHANA, TOGO, LIBERIA, **18,670**, **11,629** SAO TOME & PRINCIPE, EQUATORIAL GUINEA, CAMEROON, GABON, CONGO, ANGO, NAMIB

In the mid-1990s, AIDS and HIV infections are still increasing dramatically. Tuberculosis, for some years in retreat and supposedly curable, is increasing sharply.

TUBERCULOSIS:
RATES OF INCREASE/DECREASE
PER 100,000 POPULATION
1989-91 compared with 1984-86

increase

50%

25%

decrease

25%

50%

no data

incidence of TB, top 12 states

Highest increases: Nepal, 5,240%; Indonesia, 783%; Egypt, 734%

12,958 ETHIOPIA
4,875
30,126 KENYA
38,719 TANZANIA
31,857 MADAGASCAR

Source: WHO.

55

The estimated value of the annual trade in futures' or derivatives' contracts ranges from U.S. $23 trillion (million million) to over six times that figure. It dwarfs the combined capital values of the world's export trade and its leading stock exchanges.

Reassurances that a market involving such enormous sums is fundamentally sound, since every contract to buy is balanced by one to sell, have proved increasingly hollow. Large industrial companies and banks have already been driven by their losses to the edge of extinction.

Source: press reports.

World trade in futures
and derivatives 1994:
U.S. $23 trillion

Value of leading stock markets 1993:
U.S. $8.8 trillion

World trade in goods 1992:
U.S. $3.7 trillion

57

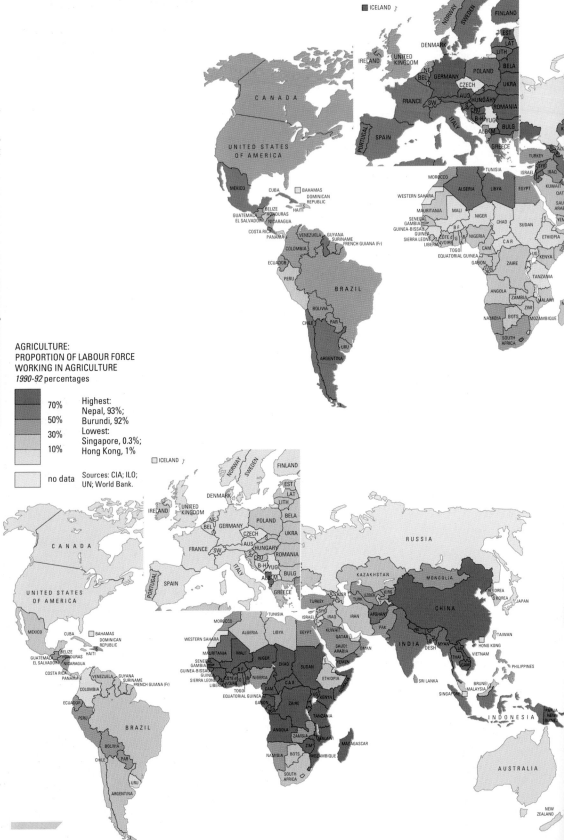

Michael Kidron and Ronald Segal *The State of the World Atlas* 5th edition   Copyright © Myriad Editions Limited

AGRICULTURE:
PROPORTION OF LABOUR FORCE
WORKING IN AGRICULTURE
1990-92 percentages

70%
50%
30%
10%

Highest:
Nepal, 93%;
Burundi, 92%
Lowest:
Singapore, 0.3%;
Hong Kong, 1%

no data   Sources: CIA; ILO;
UN; World Bank.

The richer the country, the more likely that people in it will work away from the land.

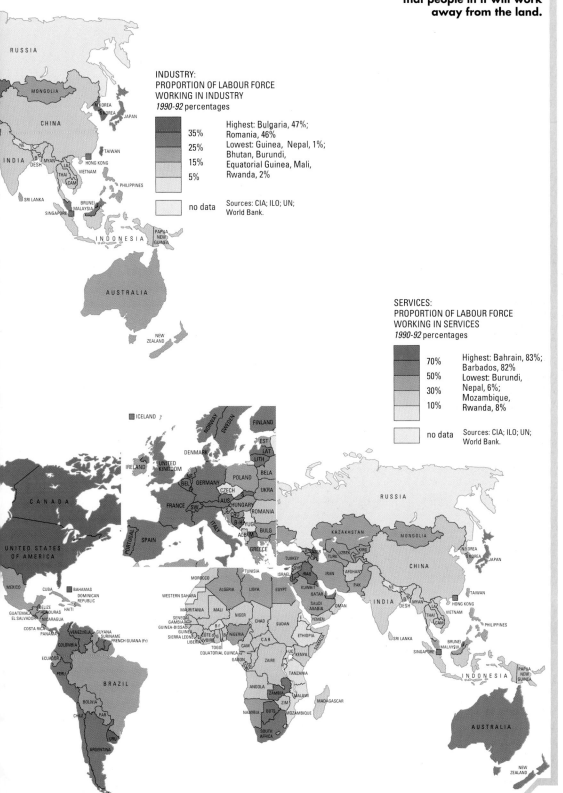

INDUSTRY:
PROPORTION OF LABOUR FORCE
WORKING IN INDUSTRY
1990-92 percentages

35%
25%
15%
5%

no data

Highest: Bulgaria, 47%;
Romania, 46%
Lowest: Guinea, Nepal, 1%;
Bhutan, Burundi,
Equatorial Guinea, Mali,
Rwanda, 2%

Sources: CIA; ILO; UN;
World Bank.

SERVICES:
PROPORTION OF LABOUR FORCE
WORKING IN SERVICES
1990-92 percentages

70%
50%
30%
10%

no data

Highest: Bahrain, 83%;
Barbados, 82%
Lowest: Burundi,
Nepal, 6%;
Mozambique,
Rwanda, 8%

Sources: CIA; ILO; UN;
World Bank.

GREENLAND
(Den)

ICELAND

CANADA

NORWAY
SWEDEN
DENMARK
UNITED
KINGDOM
IRELAND
NETH
BEL
GERMANY
POLAN
CZECH
AUS
HU
FRANCE
S
ITALY
PORTUGAL   SPAIN

UNITED STATES
OF AMERICA

MEXICO

BAHAMAS

CUBA
DOMINICAN
REPUBLIC
BELIZE   JAMAICA
HONDURAS   HAITI
GUATEMALA
EL SALVADOR
NICARAGUA
COSTA RICA
PANAMA

ATLANTIC
OCEAN

BARBADOS
TRINIDAD & TOBAGO

MOROCCO
TUNISIA
ALGERIA
LIB
WESTERN SAHARA
MAURITANIA
MALI
NIGER
CH
SENEGAL
GAMBIA
GUINEA-BISSAU
GUINEA
BURKINA
FASO
SIERRA LEONE
CÔTE d'
IVOIRE
GHANA
BENIN
NIGERIA
LIBERIA
TOGO
C
CAMEROON
EQUATORIAL GUINEA
GABON
CONGO
Z

VENEZUELA
GUYANA
SURINAME
FRENCH GUIANA (Fr)
COLOMBIA

ECUADOR

PACIFIC
OCEAN

PERU

BRAZIL

BOLIVIA
PARAGUAY
CHILE

URUGUAY

ARGENTINA

ANGOL

NAMIBIA

RELATIVE EXPLOITATION:
PAYMENT RECEIVED BY WORKERS IN
PROPORTION TO WEALTH THEY PRODUCE
1992 percentages

20%
40%
60%
80%

no data

Highest: Niger, 93.7%; Rwanda, 93.4%
Lowest: Central African Republic, 14.7%; Trinidad & Tobago, 30.4%

Sources: ICFTU; World Bank.

VALUE SUBTRACTED 22

Workers produce more wealth than they receive. The difference,
after material costs have been met, is the value subtracted
by capital - or the degree of exploitation.

RUSSIA

KAZAKHSTAN

MONGOLIA

GEO
AZER
UZBEKISTAN
KIRGISTAN
N.KOREA
JAPAN
TURKEY
TURKMEN
S.KOREA
SYRIA
DEB
TAJ
CHINA
AEL
IRAQ
JOR
IRAN
AFGHANISTAN
KUWAIT
PAKISTAN
BAHRAIN
NEPAL
BHUTAN
TAIWAN
QATAR
UAE
B.
DESH
HONG KONG
PT
SAUDI ARABIA
OMAN
INDIA
MYANMAR
LAOS
ERITREA
YEMEN
VIETNAM
AN
DJIBOUTI
THAILAND
ETHIOPIA
SOMALIA
CAM
PHILIPPINES
UGANDA
KENYA
BRUNEI
SRI LANKA
MALAYSIA
SEYCHELLES
SINGAPORE
TANZANIA
INDONESIA
PAPUA
NEW
GUINEA
MALAWI
MADAGASCAR
VE
MAURITIUS
MOZAMBIQUE

PACIFIC
OCEAN

AUSTRALIA

FIJI

In 1994
a German textile
multinational was paying children in
the Philippines 80 centavos for making a
piece of clothing that the company sold for
the equivalent of 150 pesos, a difference of
over 1,000 percent.

NEW
ZEALAND

C A N A D A

UNITED STATES
OF AMERICA

MEXICO

BAHAMAS
CUBA
DOMINICAN REPUBLIC
BELIZE   JAMAICA   HAITI
GUATEMALA   HONDURAS   PUERTO RICO
EL SALVADOR   ANTIGUA & BARBUDA
NICARAGUA   GUADELOUPE (Fr)
COSTA RICA   ST LUCIA
PANAMA   BARBADOS
   TRINIDAD & TOBAGO
VENEZUELA
GUYANA
COLOMBIA   SURINAME
   FRENCH GUIANA (Fr)
ECUADOR

ATLANTIC
OCEAN

PACIFIC
OCEAN

PERU
BRAZIL

BOLIVIA

PARAGUAY

CHILE

URUGUAY

ARGENTINA

ICELAND
NORWAY   FINLAN
SWEDEN
   ESTON
   LATVI
IRELAND   DENMARK   LITHUANIA
UNITED   NETH   POLAND   BELA
KINGDOM   BEL   GERMANY   UKRA
   CZECH   ROMA
   REPUBLIC   SLOVAK
FRANCE   SWITZ   AUSTRIA   HUNGARY
   SLO   CROATIA   YUG
   B-H
PORTUGAL   ITALY   ALB   BULG
SPAIN   M
   GREECE

MOROCCO   TUNISIA
   ALGERIA   LIB
WESTERN SAHARA
MAURITANIA   MALI   NIGER
SENEGAL   BURKINA   CH
GAMBIA   FASO
GUINEA-BISSAU   GUINEA   BENIN   NIGERIA
SIERRA LEONE   CÔTE d'   GHANA   CAMEROON   C
LIBERIA   IVOIRE   TOGO
   EQUATORIAL GUINEA
   GABON
   CONGO   ANGO
   NAMIBIA

**TRADE UNION MEMBERSHIP AS A
PROPORTION OF THE LABOUR FORCE**
1992 or latest available date

60%
40%
20%
10%

no trade unions

no data

**PROPORTION OF WORKERS
INVOLVED IN STRIKES OR LOCKOUTS**
1992 or latest available date

more than 10% involved in strikes or lockouts

1.1% to 10% involved in strikes or lockouts

0.1% to 1.0% involved in strikes or lockouts

Sources: ILO; Europa World Yearbooks; CIA *World Factbook 1993;*
World Bank; U.S. State Department.

CONDITIONS OF TRADE UNIONISM *early 1990s*

banned or otherwise absent

wholly or mainly controlled by the governing

seriously restricted and/or harrassed

newly free

traditionally free

no data

Sources: ILO; Europa World Yearbooks; CIA *World
Factbook 1993;* World Bank; U.S. State Department.

Free trade unions are an essential test of a democratic society. There are
many societies, professing to be democratic, which do not pass it.

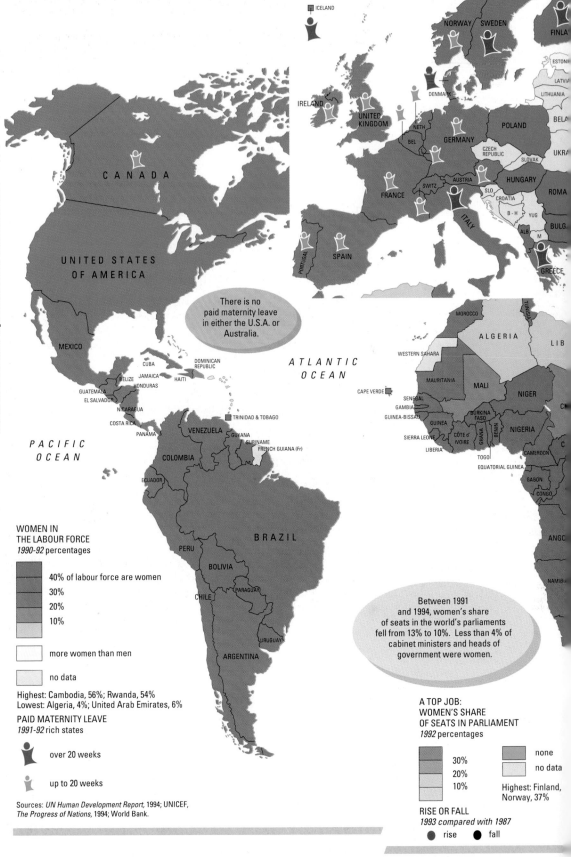

ICELAND

NORWAY   SWEDEN   FINLA

ESTONI

LATVIA

LITHUANIA

IRELAND

DENMARK

BELA

UNITED
KINGDOM

NETH

POLAND

UKRA

BEL

GERMANY

CZECH
REPUBLIC   SLOVAK

C A N A D A

FRANCE

SWITZ

AUSTRIA

HUNGARY

ROMA

SLO

CROATIA

B - H   YUG

BULG

ITALY

ALB

M

PORTUGAL

SPAIN

GREECE

UNITED STATES
OF AMERICA

There is no
paid maternity leave
in either the U.S.A. or
Australia.

MOROCCO

TUNISIA

ALGERIA

LIB

WESTERN SAHARA

MEXICO

CUBA

DOMINICAN
REPUBLIC

*A T L A N T I C
O C E A N*

MAURITANIA

MALI

NIGER

BELIZE

JAMAICA

HAITI

CAPE VERDE

GUATEMALA

HONDURAS

SENEGAL

EL SALVADOR

GAMBIA

C

NICARAGUA

GUINEA-BISSAU

BURKINA
FASO

BENIN

NIGERIA

COSTA RICA

TRINIDAD & TOBAGO

GUINEA

CÔTE d'
IVOIRE

GHANA

PANAMA

VENEZUELA

GUYANA

SIERRA LEONE

*P A C I F I C
O C E A N*

SURINAME

LIBERIA

TOGO

CAMEROON

FRENCH GUIANA (Fr)

EQUATORIAL GUINEA

COLOMBIA

GABON

CONGO

ECUADOR

B R A Z I L

ANGO

PERU

BOLIVIA

NAMIBI

CHILE

PARAGUAY

Between 1991
and 1994, women's share
of seats in the world's parliaments
fell from 13% to 10%. Less than 4% of
cabinet ministers and heads of
government were women.

URUGUAY

ARGENTINA

WOMEN IN
THE LABOUR FORCE
1990-92 percentages

- 40% of labour force are women
- 30%
- 20%
- 10%

more women than men

no data

Highest: Cambodia, 56%; Rwanda, 54%
Lowest: Algeria, 4%; United Arab Emirates, 6%

PAID MATERNITY LEAVE
1991-92 rich states

over 20 weeks

up to 20 weeks

A TOP JOB:
WOMEN'S SHARE
OF SEATS IN PARLIAMENT
1992 percentages

- 30%
- 20%
- 10%

no data

Highest: Finland,
Norway, 37%

RISE OR FALL
1993 compared with 1987
● rise   ● fall

Sources: *UN Human Development Report,* 1994; UNICEF,
The Progress of Nations, 1994; World Bank.

In most states fewer women than men are in paid work.
Most of the top jobs still go to men.

Sources: *UN Human Development Report*, 1994; UNICEF,
The Progress of Nations, 1994.

ICELAND

CANADA

UNITED STATES
OF AMERICA

40%
MEXICO

ATLANTIC
OCEAN

BAHAMAS

CUBA
DOMINICAN
REPUBLIC
HAITI

BELIZE
JAMAICA
GUATEMALA
HONDURAS
30-40% EL SALVADOR
NICARAGUA   **50%**
COSTA RICA
PANAMA

GRENADA   BARBADOS
TRINIDAD & TOBAGO   **35%**

PACIFIC
OCEAN

VENEZUELA
GUYANA
SURINAME
FRENCH GUIANA (Fr)

COLOMBIA

55%
ECUADOR

70%

BRAZIL

PERU

BOLIVIA

PARAGUAY

CHILE

URUGUAY

ARGENTINA

NORWAY   SWEDEN   FINLAND

DEN
UNITED
KINGDOM
IRELAND

NETH
BEL   GERMANY
FRANCE
ITALY
PORTUGAL   SPAIN

EST
LAT
LITH
BELARUS
POLAND
CZ   SLO
AUS   HUNG   UKRAINE
S
S   C   ROMANIA   MOL
B-H   YUG
ALB   BULG
M
TU

MOROCCO   TUNISIA
WESTERN SAHARA   ALGERIA   LIB

CAPE VERDE
MAURITANIA   MALI   NIGER
SENEGAL
GAMBIA   BURKINA
GUINEA-BISSAU   FASO   NIGERIA
GUINEA   BENIN
SIERRA LEONE   CÔTE d'   GHANA   C
IVOIRE   TOGO
LIBERIA   CAMEROON   C
EQUATORIAL GUINEA

GABON
CONGO

ANGO

NAMIB

PROPORTION OF LABOUR FORCE UNEMPLOYED
1993 or latest available date percentages

- 20%
- 15%
- 10%
- 5%
- no data

Highest proportion unemployed: Mozambique, 50%;
South Africa, 45%; Jordan, 40%; Algeria, Lebanon, 35%;
Haiti, 25-50%

high underemployment
percentages of labour force where known

high labour exporters
percentages of labour force where known

Sources: *CIA; Europa Regional Yearbooks; Facts
and Figures Annual;* ILO; Karasik; UN; World Bank.

Unemployment is endemic in poor states and rising in rich ones. Underemployment is rising, too. Many people migrate abroad to seek work.

RUSSIA

KAZAKHSTAN

MONGOLIA

N KOREA · JAPAN
S KOREA

UZBEKISTAN · KIRGISTAN
TURKMEN · TAJIKISTAN

CHINA

AZER
IRAQ · IRAN · AFGHANISTAN
JOR
KUWAIT · PAKISTAN
BAHRAIN
QATAR · UAE
SAUDI ARABIA · OMAN

ERITREA · YEMEN
DJIBOUTI

ETHIOPIA · SOMALIA

ANDA
KENYA

ANZANIA

COMOROS

MALAWI

MADAGASCAR

MOZAMBIQUE

MAURITIUS

SEYCHELLES

25-40%

NEPAL · BHUTAN
B DESH
INDIA · MYANMAR · LAOS · VIETNAM
THAILAND
CAM

TAIWAN
HONG KONG

22%
PHILIPPINES

MALDIVES · SRI LANKA

MALAYSIA · BRUNEI
SINGAPORE

INDONESIA
45%

PAPUA NEW GUINEA

PACIFIC OCEAN

AUSTRALIA

FIJI

NEW ZEALAND

THE SEARCH FOR WORK: ARRIVALS AND DEPARTURES OF MIGRANTS *1993*

- more arrivals than departures
- arrivals and departures balance
- more departures than arrivals
- no data

60% of men

GREENLAND (Den)
CANADA
UNITED STATES OF AMERICA
RUSSIA
KAZAKHSTAN · MONGOLIA
TURKEY · CHINA · JAPAN
IRAN
ALGERIA · LIBYA · INDIA
SUDAN
BRAZIL · ZAIRE
INDONESIA
AUSTRALIA

Source: CIA.

THE WORLD'S TOP 100 TRANSNATIONALS *1990*
Shares of total sales by headquarters state,
percentages

Total sales in 1990: $3,100 billion

Sources: UN, *World Investment Report:
Transnational Corporations*, 1993;
World Resources Institute, *World Resources 1994-95.*

Norway 0.3

Netherlands/UK 4.7%

Netherlands 1.3%

UK 5.5%

Belgium 0.8%

Switzerland 3.1%

Canada 0.6%

France 8.3%

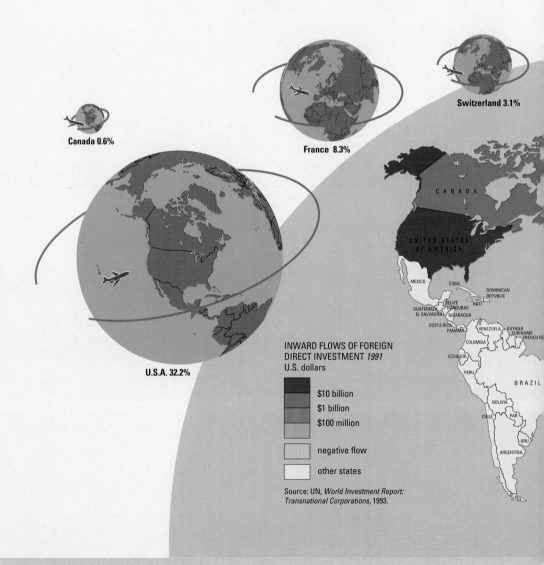

U.S.A. 32.2%

CANADA

UNITED STATES
OF AMERICA

MEXICO   CUBA
                              DOMINICAN
                              REPUBLIC
          BELIZE   HAITI
GUATEMALA HONDURAS
EL SALVADOR NICARAGUA
       COSTA RICA
          PANAMA   VENEZUELA   GUYANA
                                SURINAME
                                FRENCH GU
                    COLOMBIA
                              ECUADOR
                    PERU
                                        BRAZIL
                              BOLIVIA
                    CHILE   PAR
                                        URU
                              ARGENTINA

INWARD FLOWS OF FOREIGN
DIRECT INVESTMENT *1991*
U.S. dollars

$10 billion
$1 billion
$100 million

negative flow

other states

Source: UN, *World Investment Report:
Transnational Corporations*, 1993.

Transnationals invest in one another's backyards. Out of 37,000 transnationals worldwide, the top 100 have sales of $3,100 billion, almost half of which comes from abroad.

Sweden 1.6%

Germany 9.1%

Italy 3.6%

Japan 28.2%

Australia 0.5%

New Zealand 0.2%

ICELAND

RUSSIA

IRELAND

DEN

SWEDEN

POL

BELS

UKRAINE

KAZAKHSTAN

MONGOLIA

GER

FRANCE

THUN

ROM

BUL

AZER

UZBEK

KIRG

N KOREA

ITALY

TURKEY

TURK

S KOREA

JAPAN

PORTUGAL

GREECE

SYR

IRAQ

IRAN

AFGHAN

CHINA

SPAIN

ISRAEL

TUNISIA

MOROCCO

KUWAIT

PAK

TAIWAN

ALGERIA

LIBYA

EGYPT

QATAR

BAHRAIN

NE

INDIA

DESH

MYAN

LAO

HONG KONG

ITANIA

MALI

NIGER

CHAD

SUDAN

SAUDI ARABIA

OMAN

YEMEN

THAI

CAM

VIETNAM

PHILIPPINES

UINEA

CÔTE D'IVOIRE

NIGERIA

C A R

ETHIOPIA

SRI LANKA

BRUNEI

TOGO

CAM

SOMALIA

MALAYSIA

EQUATORIAL GUINEA

GABON

UG

KENYA

SINGAPORE

ZAIRE

TANZANIA

I N D O N E S I A

PAPUA NEW GUINEA

ANGOLA

SOLOMON ISLANDS

ZAMBIA

MALAWI

WESTERN SAMOA

NAMIBIA

BOTS

ZIM

MOZAMBIQUE

MADAGASCAR

VANUATU

FIJI

SOUTH AFRICA

A U S T R A L I A

NEW ZEALAND

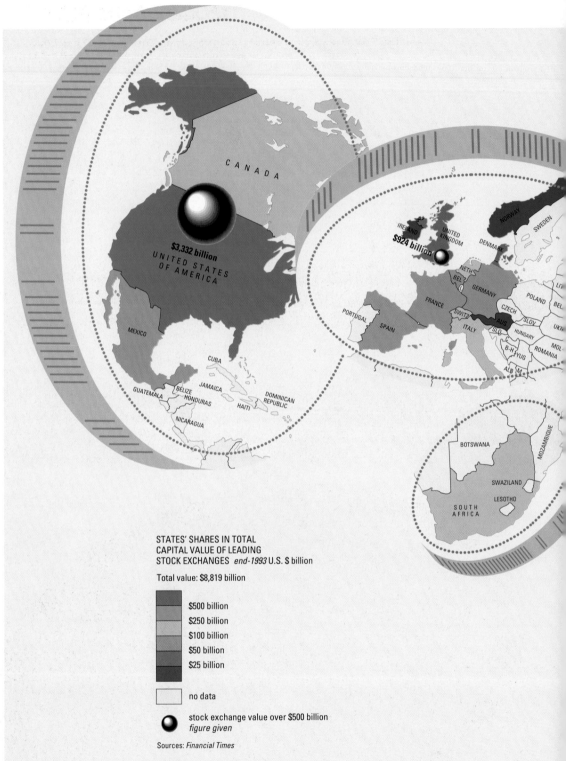

CANADA

UNITED STATES OF AMERICA

$3,332 billion

MEXICO

GUATEMALA   BELIZE
HONDURAS

CUBA

JAMAICA

HAITI

DOMINICAN
REPUBLIC

NICARAGUA

IRELAND   UNITED
KINGDOM

$924 billion

NORWAY

SWEDEN

DENMARK

PORTUGAL   SPAIN

FRANCE

NETH
BEL   GERMANY

SWITZ
ITALY

CZECH

POLAND

LIT
BEL

SLOV
SLO   HUNGARY

AUS

UKR

B-H YUG

ROMANIA

MOL

ALB M

BOTSWANA

MOZAMBIQUE

SWAZILAND

LESOTHO

SOUTH
AFRICA

STATES' SHARES IN TOTAL
CAPITAL VALUE OF LEADING
STOCK EXCHANGES *end-1993* U.S. $ billion

Total value: $8,819 billion

	$500 billion
	$250 billion
	$100 billion
	$50 billion
	$25 billion
	no data

● stock exchange value over $500 billion
figure given

Sources: *Financial Times*

The line between investment and speculation has always been blurred. It is becoming more and more threateningly so.

$2,271 billion

N KOREA
S KOREA
CHINA
JAPAN
HONG KONG
TAIWAN
VIETNAM
MALAYSIA
SINGAPORE
PHILIPPINES
PACIFIC OCEAN
PAPUA NEW GUINEA
AUSTRALIA
NEW ZEALAND

STATES' SHARES OF TOTAL TRADE
IN FUTURES AND DERIVATIVES
1992 percentage given

RISE OR FALL IN STATES' SHARES
1992-93

75% rise
50%
25%

25% fall

Sources: *Financial Times; The Economist.*

Japan 11.4%
Germany 4.8%
Malaysia 1.1%
Singapore 1.7%
Brazil 4.8%
U.S.A. 48.5%
UK 14.7%
Netherlands 0.53%
Switzerland 2.4%
Sweden 2.4%
France 7.6%
Australia 2.4%

ICELAND

NORWAY · SWEDEN · FINLAND

IRELAND · UNITED KINGDOM · DENMARK · ESTONIA · LATVIA · LITHUANIA

NETH · POLAND · BELA

BEL · GERMANY · CZECH REPUBLIC · SLOVAK · UKRA

FRANCE · SWITZ · AUSTRIA · HUNGARY · ROMA

SLO · CROATIA · B - H · YUG · BULG

ITALY · ALB · M · GREECE

C A N A D A

UNITED STATES OF AMERICA

BERMUDA

MEXICO

BEL
GUATEMALA
EL SALVADOR
HONDURAS
NICARAGUA
COSTA RICA
PANAMA

PACIFIC OCEAN

CAYMAN ISLANDS

BAHAMAS

CUBA

JAMAICA · HAITI

DOMINICAN REPUBLIC

PUERTO RICO

HAITI

VIRGIN ISLANDS
ANGUILLA
ANTIGUA & BARBUDA
ST. KITTS NEVIS
MONTSERRAT
GUADELOUPE (Fr)
DOMINICA
MARTINIQUE (Fr)
ST. LUCIA
ST. VINCENT & GRENADINES
BARBADOS
GRENADA

CAPE VERDE

TRINIDAD & TOBAGO

VENEZUELA
GUYANA
SURINAME
FRENCH GUIANA (Fr)

COLOMBIA

ECUADOR

PERU

B R A Z I L

BOLIVIA

PARAGUAY

CHILE

URUGUAY

ARGENTINA

MOROCCO
WESTERN SAHARA
ALGERIA · TUNISIA · LIB
MAURITANIA · MALI · NIGER
SENEGAL
GAMBIA
GUINEA-BISSAU
GUINEA
SIERRA LEONE
LIBERIA
CÔTE d'IVOIRE
GHANA
BURKINA FASO
BENIN
TOGO
NIGERIA
CAMEROON
EQUATORIAL GUINEA
GABON
CONGO
CH
ANGO
NAMIBI

STATES' MAIN ROLE IN GLOBAL PROHIBITED DRUG NETWORK
1993

- drug producer
- drug processor
- conduit for drugs and/or processor chemicals
- drug consumer

- no data or insignificant

- business centres for top level negotiations

- states whose role in the drug network makes them essential to the industry

- major drug money laundering sites

Source: U.S. State Department.

Authority everywhere tries to stamp itself on women's bodies.

BEHIND CLOSED DOORS:
WIFE-BEATING AND MARITAL RAPE
early 1990s

- reported as widespread
- reported as significant
- reported as rare
- no data

Sources: U.S. Department of State; authors' judgement.

ICELAND

NORWAY

SWEDEN

FINLA

DENMARK

ESTO

LATV

LITHUANIA

IRELAND

UNITED
KINGDOM

NETH

BEL

POLAND

BEL

GERMANY

UKR

CZECH
REPUBLIC

SLOVAK

FRANCE

SWITZ

AUSTRIA

HUNGARY

SLO

ROMAN

CROATIA

B - H

YUG

BUL

PORTUGAL

SPAIN

ITALY

ALB

M

GREECE

CANADA

UNITED STATES
OF AMERICA

MEXICO

BAHAMAS

CUBA

HAITI

DOMINICAN
REPUBLIC

JAMAICA

BELIZE

GUATEMALA

HONDURAS

EL SALVADOR

NICARAGUA

COSTA RICA

PANAMA

GRENADA

TRINIDAD & TOBAGO

VENEZUELA

GUYANA

SURINAME

FRENCH GUIANA (Fr)

COLOMBIA

ECUADOR

*ATLANTIC
OCEAN*

MOROCCO

ALGERIA

TUNISIA

LI

WESTERN SAHARA

CAPE VERDE

MAURITANIA

MALI

NIGER

SENEGAL

GAMBIA

GUINEA-
BISSAU

GUINEA

BURKINA
FASO

BENIN

NIGERIA

C

SIERRA LEONE

CÔTE d'
IVOIRE

GHANA

LIBERIA

TOGO

EQUATORIAL
GUINEA

CAMEROON

CA

SAO TOME
& PRINCIPE

GABON

GABON

CONGO

BRAZIL

PERU

BOLIVIA

CHILE

PARAGUAY

URUGUAY

ARGENTINA

ANGO

NAMIE

9.8	U.S.A.
8.1	Denmark
7.4	Japan
6.9	New Zealand
6.2	Finland
5.7	Hungary
5.5	Australia
4.9	Switzerland
4.7	Bulgaria
4.3	Austria, Belgium
3.9	U.K.
3.5	Germany
3.1	France
2.7	Canada
2.4	Poland
2.1	Netherlands
1.7	Norway
0.9	Sweden
0.4	Italy
0.2	Spain

INFANT DEATHS
FROM PRESUMED ABUSE
per 100,000 live births *1994*
selected countries

Source: UNICEF.

CHILD LABOUR:
MINIMUM AGE OF LEGAL EMPLOYMENT
1993

- 12 years or no legal minimum
- 13 years
- 14 years
- 15 years
- 16 years or over
- no data

minimum age limit rarely enforced,
especially in agriculture and informal
economy

Sources: International Confederation of Free Trade
Unions; U.S. State Department.

Children are widely exploited, not least for their labour.

RUSSIA

KAZAKHSTAN

MONGOLIA

N.KOREA

JAPAN

S KOREA

UZBEKISTAN

KIRGISTAN

TURKMEN

TAJ.

URKEY

GEO

AZER

SYRIA

EB

IRAQ

IRAN

AFGHANISTAN

PAKISTAN

CHINA

EL

JOR

KUWAIT

BAHRAIN

QATAR

UAE

OMAN

SAUDI ARABIA

YEMEN

ERITREA

DJIBOUTI

ETHIOPIA

SOMALIA

NEPAL

BHUTAN

B
DESH

INDIA

MYANMAR

LAOS

THAI

CAM

VIETNAM

TAIWAN

HONG KONG

*PACIFIC
OCEAN*

PHILIPPINES

KIRIBATI

MALDIVES

SRI LANKA

BRUNEI

MALAYSIA

SINGAPORE

INDONESIA

PAPUA
NEW
GUINEA

SOLOMON
ISLANDS

UGANDA

KENYA

TANZANIA

COMOROS

MALAWI

MADAGASCAR

MAURITIUS

MOZAMBIQUE

WESTERN SAMOA

FIJI

AUSTRALIA

NEW
ZEALAND

**REPORTED SEXUAL ABUSE
OF CHILDREN BY FOREIGN
BUSINESSMEN OR TOURISTS** *1994*

Latin America	**Africa**	**Asia**
Argentina	Benin	Bangladesh
Brazil	Côte d'Ivoire	Cambodia
Chile	Guinea	India
Colombia	Kenya	Indonesia
Costa Rica	Mali	S Korea
Cuba	Mauritania	Pakistan
Dominican	Morocco	Philippines
Republic	Senegal	Sri Lanka
El Salvador	Zaire	Taiwan
Guatemala		Thailand
Haiti		Vietnam
Mexico		
Peru		
Uruguay	Source: UNICEF.	

**NUMBER OF
CHILD PROSTITUTES** *1994*
India 300,000
Philippines, Taiwan, Thailand 100,000
Pakistan, Vietnam 40,000
Sri Lanka 30,000

Source: UNICEF.

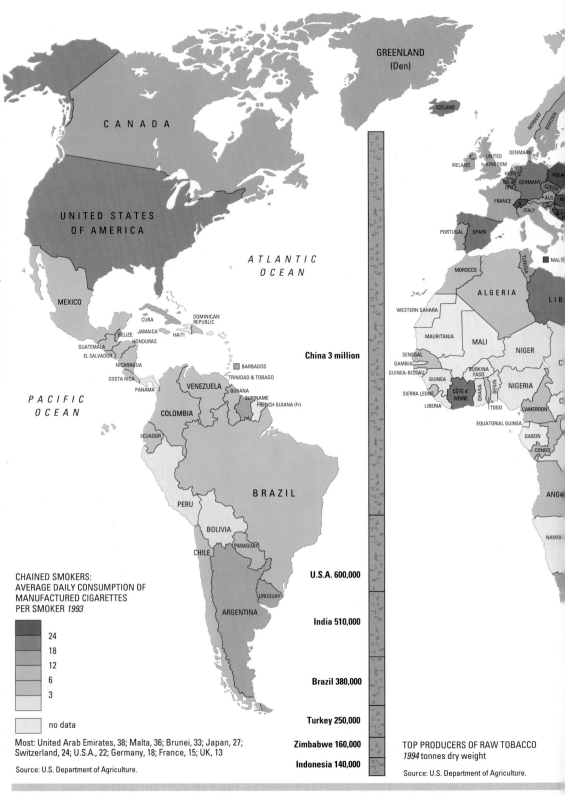

GREENLAND
(Den)

ICELAND

NORWAY SWEDEN

DENMARK
IRELAND UNITED
KINGDOM

NETH   POLA
BEL &   GERMANY   CZECH
LUX   AUS   H

FRANCE   ITALY   B

PORTUGAL   SPAIN

MALT

MOROCCO

TUNISIA

ALGERIA

LIB

WESTERN SAHARA

MAURITANIA   MALI   NIGER

SENEGAL
GAMBIA   BURKINA
GUINEA-BISSAU   FASO

GUINEA   NIGERIA

SIERRA LEONE   CÔTE d'
                IVOIRE   GHANA   BENIN

LIBERIA   TOGO   CAMEROON

EQUATORIAL GUINEA

GABON
CONGO

ANG

NAMIB

CANADA

**UNITED STATES
OF AMERICA**

MEXICO

CUBA

BELIZE   JAMAICA
GUATEMALA   HONDURAS
EL SALVADOR

NICARAGUA

COSTA RICA

PANAMA

DOMINICAN
REPUBLIC

HAITI

BARBADOS

TRINIDAD & TOBAGO

VENEZUELA   GUYANA
            SURINAME
            FRENCH GUIANA (Fr)

COLOMBIA

ECUADOR

PERU

BRAZIL

BOLIVIA

PARAGUAY

CHILE

URUGUAY

ARGENTINA

*ATLANTIC
OCEAN*

*PACIFIC
OCEAN*

China 3 million

U.S.A. 600,000

India 510,000

Brazil 380,000

Turkey 250,000

Zimbabwe 160,000

Indonesia 140,000

CHAINED SMOKERS:
AVERAGE DAILY CONSUMPTION OF
MANUFACTURED CIGARETTES
PER SMOKER *1993*

24
18
12
6
3

no data

Most: United Arab Emirates, 38; Malta, 36; Brunei, 33; Japan, 27;
Switzerland, 24; U.S.A., 22; Germany, 18; France, 15; UK, 13

Source: U.S. Department of Agriculture.

TOP PRODUCERS OF RAW TOBACCO
1994 tonnes dry weight

Source: U.S. Department of Agriculture.

Each day, between 1.3 and 1.4 billion people consume more than 17,000 tonnes of tobacco.

"One tonne of tobacco = one million cigarettes = one death"
Richard Peto, 1993

RUSSIA

KAZAKHSTAN

MONGOLIA

GEO
AZER
UZBEKISTAN
KIRGISTAN
URKEY
TURKMEN
TAJ.
SYRIA
LEB
IRAQ
IRAN
AFGHANISTAN
EL
JOR
KUWAIT
PAKISTAN
BAHRAIN
QATAR
UAE
SAUDI ARABIA
OMAN

N KOREA
JAPAN
S KOREA

CHINA

NEPAL
BHUTAN
B
DESH
INDIA
MYANMAR
LAOS
VIETNAM

TAIWAN

HONG KONG

PACIFIC OCEAN

THAILAND
CAM

PHILIPPINES

ERITREA
YEMEN
DJIBOUTI

ETHIOPIA
SOMALIA

SRI LANKA

BRUNEI

MALAYSIA

GANDA
KENYA

SEYCHELLES

TANZANIA

INDONESIA

PAPUA NEW GUINEA

SOLOMON ISLANDS

MALAWI

MADAGASCAR

MAURITIUS

MOZAMBIQUE

WESTERN SAMOA

AUSTRALIA

FIJI

NEW ZEALAND

Exporters

Importers

Brazil 230,000

U.S.A. 200,000

Zimbabwe 190,000

Turkey 130,000

Greece 110,000

Italy 100,000

Malawi 100,000

200,000 U.S.A.

180,000 Germany

130,000 UK

125,000 Russia

120,000 Japan

90,000 Netherlands

50,000 Spain

TOP TRADERS IN RAW TOBACCO
1994 tonnes dry weight

Source: U.S. Department of Agriculture.

ICELAND

NORWAY
SWEDEN
FINLAN
ESTONI
LATVI
LITHUANIA
DENMARK
IRELAND
UNITED
KINGDOM
NETH
BEL
11,179
GERMANY
POLAND
BEL
CZECH
REPUBLIC
UKR
SLOVAK
30,003
FRANCE
SWITZ
AUSTRIA
HUNGARY
ROMA
SLO
CROATIA
21,770
ITALY
B · H
YUG
BULG
ALB
M
PORTUGAL
24,202
SPAIN
GREECE

C A N A D A

411,907

U N I T E D   S T A T E S
O F   A M E R I C A

BERMUDA

ATLANTIC
OCEAN

MOROCCO
TUNISIA
ALGERIA
LIB
WESTERN SAHARA

18,353
MEXICO

BAHAMAS
CUBA
DOMINICAN
REPUBLIC
JAMAICA
BELIZE
HAITI
ANGUILLA
ANTIGUA & BARBUDA
ST KITTS NEVIS
GUADELOUPE
GUATEMALA
HONDURAS
DOMINICA
EL SALVADOR
MARTINIQUE
ST LUCIA
NETHERLANDS
ANTILLES
ST. VINCENT &
GRENADINES
BARBADOS
NICARAGUA
GRENADA
TRINIDAD & TOBAGO
COSTA RICA
PANAMA
VENEZUELA
GUYANA
SURINAME
FRENCH GUIANA (Fr)

CAPE VERDE

MAURITANIA
MALI
NIGER
SENEGAL
GAMBIA
GUINEA-BISSAU
GUINEA
BURKINA
FASO
NIGERIA
SIERRA LEONE
CÔTE d'
IVOIRE
GHANA
BENIN
LIBERIA
TOGO
CAMEROON
EQUATORIAL
GUINEA
18,670
11,629
SAO TOME &
PRINCIPE
GABON
CONGO

C

PACIFIC
OCEAN

COLOMBIA

ECUADOR

PERU

49,312

B R A Z I L

ANGO

NAMI

BOLIVIA

AIDS
REPORTED RATES OF AIDS
PER 100,000 POPULATION
1992 or latest available data

PARAGUAY

CHILE

URUGUAY

ARGENTINA

50 per 100,000
25
15
5
1

no cases reported

no data

Highest rate per 100,000: Bahamas, 104;
Namibia, 103; Congo, 85

more than 10,000 AIDS cases
reported to March 1994 *numbers given*

Source: WHO.

HIV-INFECTED ADULTS
20m
13-14m

HIV-RELATED DEATHS
OF ADULTS
8m
2m

by 1994   by 2000   by 1994   by 2000

Source: WHO.

In the mid-1990s, AIDS and HIV infections are still increasing dramatically. Tuberculosis, for some years in retreat and supposedly curable, is increasing sharply.

TUBERCULOSIS:
RATES OF INCREASE/DECREASE
PER 100,000 POPULATION
1989-91 compared with 1984-86

increase	decrease	no data
50%	25%	
25%	50%	incidence of TB, top 12 states

Highest increases: Nepal, 5,240%; Indonesia, 783%; Egypt, 734%

12,958 ETHIOPIA
,875
30,126 KENYA
38,719 TANZANIA
4
31,857 MADAGASCAR

Source: WHO.

55

The estimated value of the annual trade in futures' or
derivatives' contracts ranges from U.S. $23 trillion
(million million) to over six times that figure. It dwarfs the
combined capital values of the world's export trade and
its leading stock exchanges.

Reassurances that a market involving such enormous
sums is fundamentally sound, since every contract to buy
is balanced by one to sell, have proved increasingly
hollow. Large industrial companies and banks have
already been driven by their losses to the edge of
extinction.

Source: press reports.

**World trade in futures
and derivatives 1994:
U.S. $23 trillion**

**Value of leading stock markets 1993:
U.S. $8.8 trillion**

**World trade in goods 1992:
U.S. $3.7 trillion**

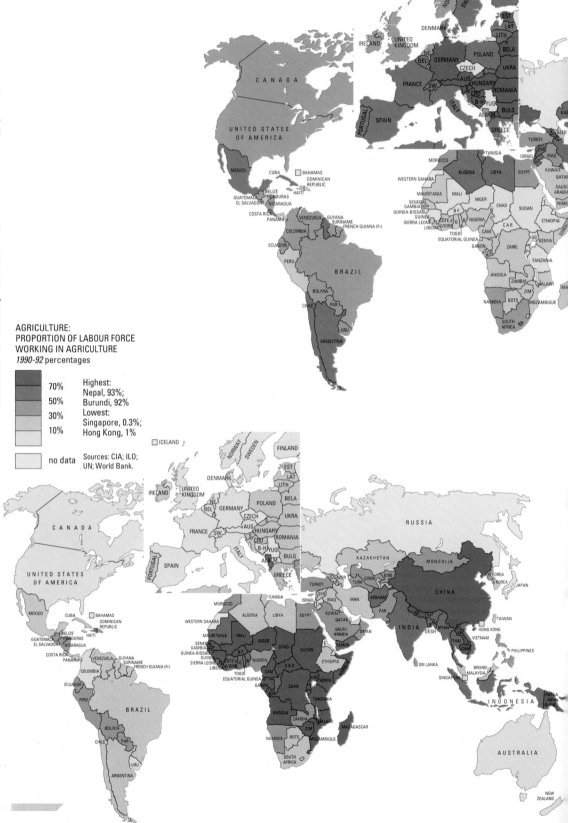

AGRICULTURE:
PROPORTION OF LABOUR FORCE
WORKING IN AGRICULTURE
1990-92 percentages

70%
50%
30%
10%

Highest:
Nepal, 93%;
Burundi, 92%
Lowest:
Singapore, 0.3%;
Hong Kong, 1%

no data

Sources: CIA; ILO;
UN; World Bank.

**The richer the country, the more likely
that people in it will work
away from the land.**

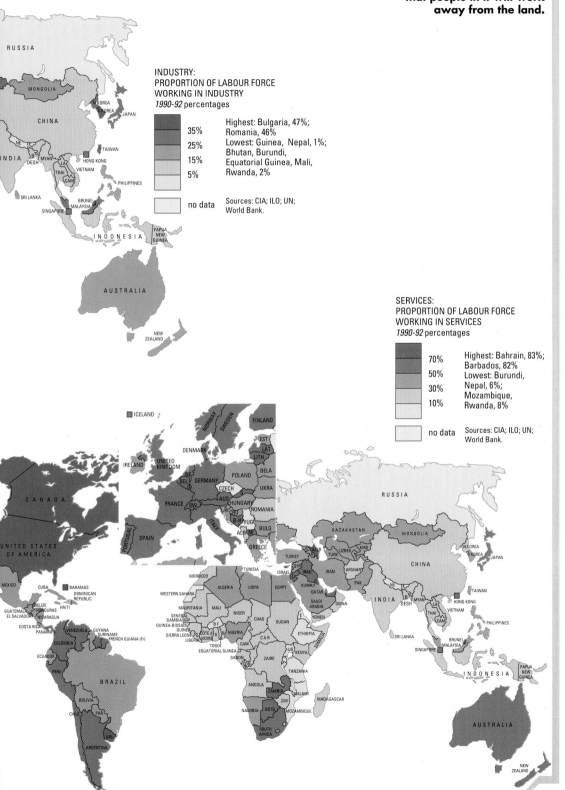

INDUSTRY:
PROPORTION OF LABOUR FORCE
WORKING IN INDUSTRY
1990-92 percentages

35%
25%
15%
5%

Highest: Bulgaria, 47%;
Romania, 46%
Lowest: Guinea, Nepal, 1%;
Bhutan, Burundi,
Equatorial Guinea, Mali,
Rwanda, 2%

no data

Sources: CIA; ILO; UN;
World Bank.

SERVICES:
PROPORTION OF LABOUR FORCE
WORKING IN SERVICES
1990-92 percentages

70%
50%
30%
10%

Highest: Bahrain, 83%;
Barbados, 82%
Lowest: Burundi,
Nepal, 6%;
Mozambique,
Rwanda, 8%

no data

Sources: CIA; ILO; UN;
World Bank.

CANADA

GREENLAND
(Den)

ICELAND

UNITED STATES
OF AMERICA

NORWAY

SWEDEN

DENMARK

IRELAND

UNITED
KINGDOM

NETH
BEL
GERMANY

POLAND

CZECH

FRANCE

S

ITALY

AUS

HU

B-H

A

GF

PORTUGAL   SPAIN

MEXICO

BAHAMAS

CUBA

BELIZE
JAMAICA
HAITI
GUATEMALA
HONDURAS
EL SALVADOR
NICARAGUA
COSTA RICA
PANAMA

DOMINICAN
REPUBLIC

ATLANTIC
OCEAN

BARBADOS
TRINIDAD & TOBAGO

MOROCCO

TUNISIA

ALGERIA

LIB

WESTERN SAHARA

MAURITANIA

MALI

NIGER

CH

SENEGAL
GAMBIA
GUINEA-BISSAU
GUINEA
SIERRA LEONE
LIBERIA

BURKINA
FASO

CÔTE d'
IVOIRE

GHANA
BENIN
TOGO

NIGERIA

CAMEROON

C

A

EQUATORIAL GUINEA

GABON

CONGO

Z

VENEZUELA

GUYANA
SURINAME
FRENCH GUIANA (Fr)

COLOMBIA

ECUADOR

PACIFIC
OCEAN

PERU

BRAZIL

BOLIVIA

PARAGUAY

CHILE

URUGUAY

ARGENTINA

ANGO

NAMIBIA

S

RELATIVE EXPLOITATION:
PAYMENT RECEIVED BY WORKERS IN
PROPORTION TO WEALTH THEY PRODUCE
1992 percentages

- 20%
- 40%
- 60%
- 80%

no data

Highest: Niger, 93.7%; Rwanda, 93.4%
Lowest: Central African Republic, 14.7%; Trinidad & Tobago, 30.4%

Sources: ICFTU; World Bank.

Workers produce more wealth than they receive. The difference, after material costs have been met, is the value subtracted by capital - or the degree of exploitation.

RUSSIA

KAZAKHSTAN

MONGOLIA

UZBEKISTAN   KIRGISTAN

TURKMEN   TAJ.

CHINA

N.KOREA   JAPAN

S KOREA

GEO

AZER

INE

TURKEY

SYRIA

LEB

IRAQ   IRAN   AFGHANISTAN

AEL   JOR

KUWAIT

BAHRAIN

PAKISTAN   NEPAL   BHUTAN

B
DESH

QATAR   UAE

PT

SAUDI ARABIA

OMAN   INDIA   MYANMAR   LAOS

VIETNAM

TAIWAN

HONG KONG

PACIFIC
OCEAN

ERITREA   YEMEN

AN   DJIBOUTI

THAILAND

CAM   PHILIPPINES

ETHIOPIA   SOMALIA

SRI LANKA   BRUNEI

UGANDA   KENYA   MALAYSIA

SINGAPORE

SEYCHELLES

TANZANIA   INDONESIA   PAPUA
NEW
GUINEA

MALAWI

MADAGASCAR

MAURITIUS

MOZAMBIQUE

VE

AUSTRALIA

FIJI

In 1994
a German textile
multinational was paying children in
the Philippines 80 centavos for making a
piece of clothing that the company sold for
the equivalent of 150 pesos, a difference of
over 1,000 percent.

NEW
ZEALAND

Michael Kidron and Ronald Segal *The State of the World Atlas* 5th edition   Copyright © Myriad Editions Limited

TRADE UNION MEMBERSHIP AS A PROPORTION OF THE LABOUR FORCE
1992 or latest available date

- 60%
- 40%
- 20%
- 10%
- no trade unions
- no data

PROPORTION OF WORKERS INVOLVED IN STRIKES OR LOCKOUTS
1992 or latest available date

more than 10% involved in strikes or lockouts

1.1% to 10% involved in strikes or lockouts

0.1% to 1.0% involved in strikes or lockouts

Sources: ILO; Europa World Yearbooks; CIA *World Factbook 1993;*
World Bank; U.S. State Department.

CONDITIONS OF TRADE UNIONISM *early 1990s*

- banned or otherwise absent
- wholly or mainly controlled by the governing
- seriously restricted and/or harrassed
- newly free
- traditionally free
- no data

Sources: ILO; Europa World Yearbooks; CIA *World
Factbook 1993;* World Bank; U.S. State Department.

Free trade unions are an essential test of a democratic society. There are many societies, professing to be democratic, which do not pass it.

ICELAND

NORWAY SWEDEN

FINLA

IRELAND

UNITED
KINGDOM

DENMARK

NETH

BEL

GERMANY

POLAND

ESTONI

LATVI

LITHUANIA

BELA

UKRA

CZECH
REPUBLIC

SLOVAK

AUSTRIA

SWITZ

HUNGARY

ROMA

SLO

CROATIA

B - H

YUG

ALB

M

BULG

GREECE

FRANCE

ITALY

PORTUGAL

SPAIN

CANADA

UNITED STATES
OF AMERICA

MEXICO

CUBA

BELIZE

JAMAICA

HAITI

DOMINICAN
REPUBLIC

GUATEMALA

HONDURAS

EL SALVADOR

NICARAGUA

COSTA RICA

PANAMA

VENEZUELA

GUYANA

SURINAME

FRENCH GUIANA (Fr)

COLOMBIA

ECUADOR

PERU

BRAZIL

BOLIVIA

PARAGUAY

CHILE

URUGUAY

ARGENTINA

PACIFIC
OCEAN

ATLANTIC
OCEAN

TRINIDAD & TOBAGO

There is no
paid maternity leave
in either the U.S.A. or
Australia.

MOROCCO

WESTERN SAHARA

CAPE VERDE

MAURITANIA

SENEGAL

GAMBIA

GUINEA-BISSAU

GUINEA

SIERRA LEONE

LIBERIA

CÔTE d'
IVOIRE

GHANA

TOGO

BENIN

MALI

ALGERIA

LIB

NIGER

BURKINA
FASO

NIGERIA

C

CAMEROON

EQUATORIAL GUINEA

GABON

CONGO

ANGO

NAMIBI

Between 1991
and 1994, women's share
of seats in the world's parliaments
fell from 13% to 10%. Less than 4% of
cabinet ministers and heads of
government were women.

Michael Kidron and Ronald Segal *The State of the World Atlas* 5th edition   Copyright © Myriad Editions Limited

WOMEN IN
THE LABOUR FORCE
1990-92 percentages

40% of labour force are women

30%

20%

10%

more women than men

no data

Highest: Cambodia, 56%; Rwanda, 54%
Lowest: Algeria, 4%; United Arab Emirates, 6%

PAID MATERNITY LEAVE
1991-92 rich states

over 20 weeks

up to 20 weeks

Sources: *UN Human Development Report,* 1994; UNICEF,
The Progress of Nations, 1994; World Bank.

A TOP JOB:
WOMEN'S SHARE
OF SEATS IN PARLIAMENT
1992 percentages

30%

20%

10%

no data

Highest: Finland,
Norway, 37%

RISE OR FALL
1993 compared with 1987

rise   fall

In most states fewer women than men are in paid work.
Most of the top jobs still go to men.

RUSSIA

KAZAKHSTAN

MONGOLIA

GEO
AZER
UZBEKISTAN
KIRGISTAN
URKEY
SYRIA
EB
TURKMEN
TAJ
N.KOREA
JAPAN

S.KOREA

IRAQ
IRAN
AFGHANISTAN
CHINA

EL
JOR
KUWAIT
PAKISTAN
BHUTAN
NEPAL

PACIFIC
OCEAN

BAHRAIN
QATAR
UAE
B
DESH
TAIWAN

SAUDI ARABIA
OMAN
INDIA
MYANMAR
LAOS
HONG KONG

MALDIVES
SRI LANKA
THAILAND
VIETNAM

N
DJIBOUTI
YEMEN
CAM
PHILIPPINES

ETHIOPIA
SOMALIA
BRUNEI

UGANDA
KENYA
SEYCHELLES
MALAYSIA
SINGAPORE

TANZANIA
COMOROS
INDONESIA
PAPUA
NEW
GUINEA

MALAWI
MADAGASCAR
MAURITIUS

OZAMBIQUE

AUSTRALIA

FIJI

ICELAND
SWEDEN
CANADA
U.K.
POLAND
FRANCE
RUSSIA
SPAIN
KAZAKHSTAN
MONGOLIA
UNITED STATES
OF AMERICA
TURKEY
CHINA
JAPAN
IRAN
ALGERIA
LIBYA
INDIA
SUDAN
BRAZIL
ZAIRE
INDONESIA
AUSTRALIA

NEW
ZEALAND

Sources: *UN Human Development Report*, 1994; UNICEF,
The Progress of Nations, 1994.

ICELAND

CANADA

UNITED STATES
OF AMERICA

40%
MEXICO

BAHAMAS

CUBA
DOMINICAN
REPUBLIC
JAMAICA BELIZE
GUATEMALA HONDURAS HAITI
30-40% EL SALVADOR
NICARAGUA **50%**
COSTA RICA GRENADA BARBADOS **35%**
PANAMA TRINIDAD & TOBAGO

ATLANTIC
OCEAN

VENEZUELA
GUYANA
SURINAME
FRENCH GUIANA (Fr)
COLOMBIA

PACIFIC
OCEAN

55% ECUADOR

70%

PERU

BRAZIL

BOLIVIA
PARAGUAY
CHILE

URUGUAY

ARGENTINA

NORWAY SWEDEN FINLAND

UNITED DEN
KINGDOM
IRELAND
EST
LAT
NETH LITH
BEL BELARUS
GERMANY POLAND
CZ SLO UKRAINE
AUS HUNG
FRANCE S MOL
S C ROMANIA
ITALY B-H YUG
ALB BULG
PORTUGAL SPAIN M TL

MOROCCO TUNISIA
WESTERN SAHARA ALGERIA LIB
CAPE VERDE MAURITANIA MALI NIGER
SENEGAL
GAMBIA BURKINA
GUINEA-BISSAU FASO BENIN NIGERIA
GUINEA CÔTE d' C
SIERRA LEONE IVOIRE GHANA
LIBERIA TOGO CAMEROON
EQUATORIAL GUINEA
GABON
CONGO

ANGO

NAMIB

PROPORTION OF LABOUR FORCE UNEMPLOYED
1993 or latest available date percentages

- 20%
- 15%
- 10%
- 5%
- no data

Highest proportion unemployed: Mozambique, 50%;
South Africa, 45%; Jordan, 40%; Algeria, Lebanon, 35%;
Haiti, 25-50%

high underemployment
percentages of labour force where known

high labour exporters
percentages of labour force where known

Sources: *CIA; Europa Regional Yearbooks; Facts
and Figures Annual;* ILO; Karasik; UN; World Bank.

Unemployment is endemic in poor states and rising in rich ones. Underemployment is rising, too. Many people migrate abroad to seek work.

RUSSIA

KAZAKHSTAN

MONGOLIA

UZBEKISTAN

KIRGISTAN

TURKMEN

TAJIKISTAN

CHINA

AZER

IRAQ

IRAN

AFGHANISTAN

25-40%

PAKISTAN

NEPAL

BHUTAN

KUWAIT

BAHRAIN

QATAR

UAE

SAUDI ARABIA

OMAN

INDIA

B
DESH

MYANMAR

LAOS

VIETNAM

HONG KONG

N.KOREA

S KOREA

JAPAN

TAIWAN

PACIFIC
OCEAN

THAILAND

CAM

ERITREA

YEMEN

DJIBOUTI

22%
PHILIPPINES

ETHIOPIA

SOMALIA

SRI LANKA

MALDIVES

BRUNEI

GANDA

KENYA

MALAYSIA

SINGAPORE

TANZANIA

SEYCHELLES

COMOROS

INDONESIA

45%

PAPUA
NEW
GUINEA

MALAWI

MADAGASCAR

MAURITIUS

THE SEARCH FOR WORK:
ARRIVALS AND DEPARTURES
OF MIGRANTS *1993*

MOZAMBIQUE

60% of
men

- more arrivals than departures
- arrivals and departures balance
- more departures than arrivals
- no data

AUSTRALIA

FIJI

NEW
ZEALAND

GREENLAND
(Den)

CANADA

RUSSIA

UNITED STATES
OF AMERICA

KAZAKHSTAN

MONGOLIA

TURKEY

JAPAN

IRAN

CHINA

ALGERIA

LIBYA

INDIA

SUDAN

BRAZIL

ZAIRE

INDONESIA

AUSTRALIA

Source: CIA.

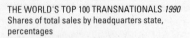

THE WORLD'S TOP 100 TRANSNATIONALS *1990*
Shares of total sales by headquarters state,
percentages

Total sales in 1990: $3,100 billion

Sources: UN, *World Investment Report:
Transnational Corporations*, 1993;
World Resources Institute, *World Resources 1994-95*.

Norway 0.3%

Netherlands/UK 4.7%

Netherlands 1.3%

UK 5.5%

Belgium 0.8%

Switzerland 3.1%

Canada 0.6%

France 8.3%

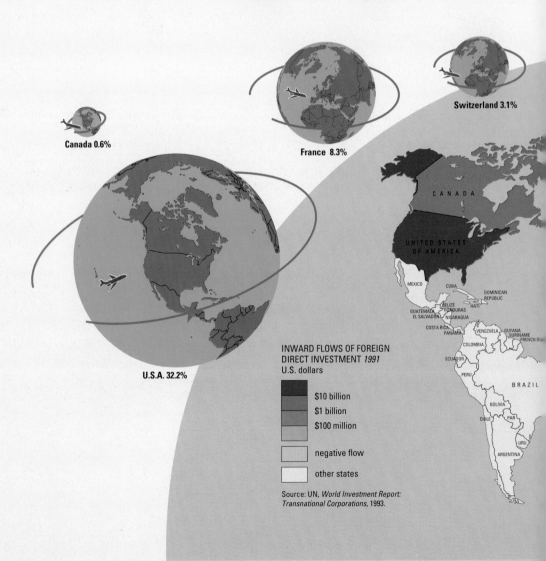

CANADA

UNITED STATES
OF AMERICA

MEXICO   CUBA
                              DOMINICAN
                              REPUBLIC
              BELIZE   HAITI
GUATEMALA HONDURAS
EL SALVADOR NICARAGUA
      COSTA RICA
            PANAMA   VENEZUELA GUYANA
                                SURINAME
                                FRENCH GUI
            COLOMBIA

            ECUADOR

            PERU

                              BRAZIL

                    BOLIVIA

            CHILE   PAR

                              URU

                    ARGENTINA

U.S.A. 32.2%

INWARD FLOWS OF FOREIGN
DIRECT INVESTMENT *1991*
U.S. dollars

$10 billion
$1 billion
$100 million

negative flow

other states

Source: UN, *World Investment Report:
Transnational Corporations*, 1993.

A GLOBAL GRASP 26

Transnationals invest in one another's backyards. Out of 37,000 transnationals worldwide, the top 100 have sales of $3,100 billion, almost half of which comes from abroad.

Sweden 1.6%

Germany 9.1%

Japan 28.2%

Italy 3.6%

Australia 0.5%

New Zealand 0.2%

ICELAND

IRELAND

PORTUGAL

MOROCCO

ALGERIA

LIBYA

EGYPT

MALI

NIGER

CHAD

SUDAN

NIGERIA

C.A.R

ETHIOPIA

CAM

GABON

ZAIRE

UG

KENYA

TANZANIA

ANGOLA

ZAMBIA

MALAWI

MADAGASCAR

NAMIBIA

BOTS

ZIM

MOZAMBIQUE

SOUTH AFRICA

RUSSIA

KAZAKHSTAN

MONGOLIA

N.KOREA

S.KOREA

JAPAN

CHINA

TURKEY

IRAN

AFGHAN

INDIA

TAIWAN

HONG KONG

VIETNAM

MYAN

THAI

PHILIPPINES

SRI LANKA

BRUNEI

MALAYSIA

SINGAPORE

INDONESIA

PAPUA NEW GUINEA

SOLOMON ISLANDS

WESTERN SAMOA

VANUATU

FIJI

AUSTRALIA

NEW ZEALAND

SAUDI ARABIA

OMAN

YEMEN

SOMALIA

KUWAIT

QATAR

BAHRAIN

IRAQ

SYR

ISRAEL

GREECE

TUNISIA

ITALY

SPAIN

FRANCE

SWEDEN

DEN

GER

POL

BEL

UKRAINE

ROM

BUL

HUN

AZER

UZBEK

KIRG

TURK

69

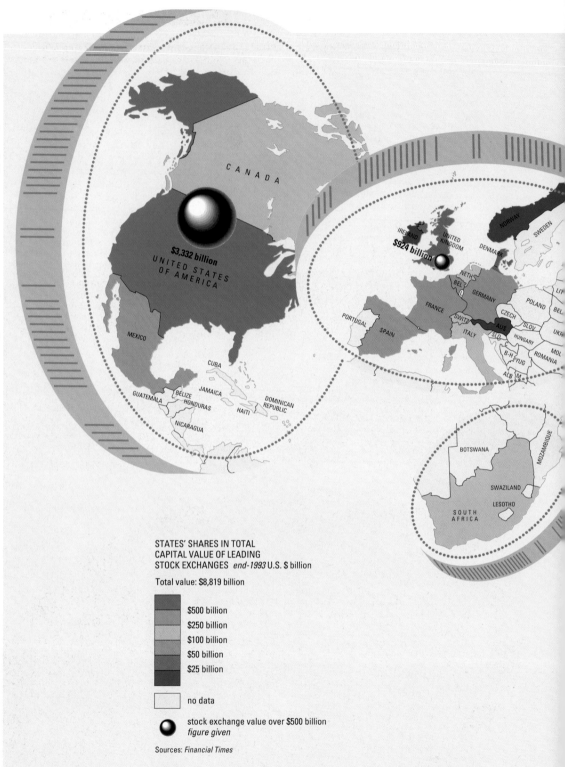

CANADA

$3,332 billion
UNITED STATES
OF AMERICA

MEXICO

CUBA

GUATEMALA · BELIZE · HONDURAS · JAMAICA · HAITI · DOMINICAN REPUBLIC

NICARAGUA

IRELAND · UNITED KINGDOM · NORWAY · SWEDEN · DENMARK

$924 billion

PORTUGAL · SPAIN · FRANCE · NETHS · BEL · GERMANY · SWITZ · ITALY · AUS · SLO · CZECH · SLOV · HUNGARY · POLAND · LIT · BEL · UKR · MOL · ROMANIA · B-H · YUG · ALB · M

BOTSWANA · MOZAMBIQUE

SWAZILAND

LESOTHO

SOUTH AFRICA

STATES' SHARES IN TOTAL
CAPITAL VALUE OF LEADING
STOCK EXCHANGES *end-1993* U.S. $ billion

Total value: $8,819 billion

- $500 billion
- $250 billion
- $100 billion
- $50 billion
- $25 billion

no data

stock exchange value over $500 billion
figure given

Sources: *Financial Times*

Michael Kidron and Ronald Segal *The State of the World Atlas* 5th edition   Copyright © Myriad Editions Limited

The line between investment and speculation has always been blurred. It is becoming more and more threateningly so.

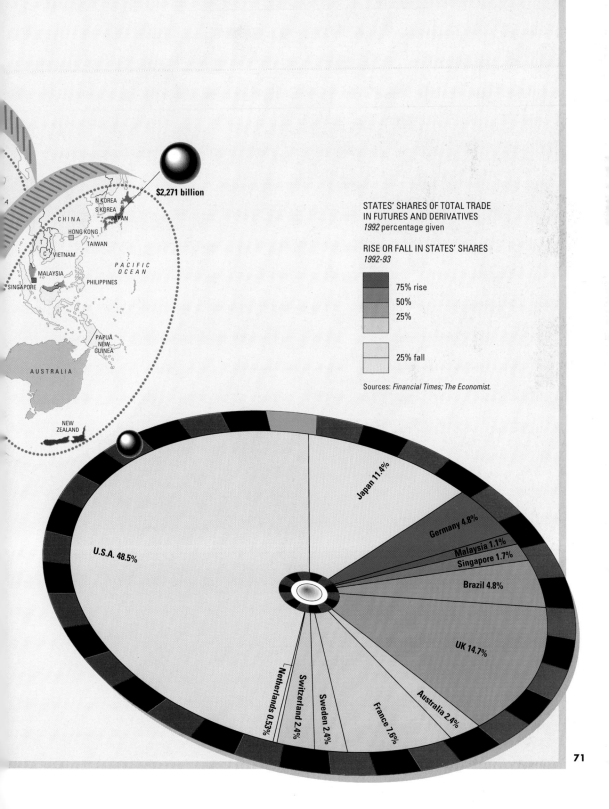

$2,271 billion

N KOREA
S KOREA
CHINA
JAPAN
HONG KONG
TAIWAN
VIETNAM
PACIFIC OCEAN
MALAYSIA
SINGAPORE
PHILIPPINES
PAPUA NEW GUINEA
AUSTRALIA
NEW ZEALAND

STATES' SHARES OF TOTAL TRADE IN FUTURES AND DERIVATIVES
1992 percentage given

RISE OR FALL IN STATES' SHARES
1992-93

75% rise
50%
25%

25% fall

Sources: *Financial Times; The Economist.*

Japan 11.4%
Germany 4.8%
Malaysia 1.1%
Singapore 1.7%
Brazil 4.8%
U.S.A. 48.5%
UK 14.7%
Australia 2.4%
France 7.6%
Sweden 2.4%
Switzerland 2.4%
Netherlands 0.53%

ICELAND

NORWAY
SWEDEN
FINLAN
ESTONI
LATVIA
LITHUANIA
DENMARK

IRELAND
UNITED
KINGDOM
NETH.
POLAND
BELA
BEL
GERMANY
CZECH
REPUBLIC
UKRA
FRANCE
SWITZ.
AUSTRIA
SLOVAK
HUNGARY
ROMA
SLO
CROATIA
B-H
YUG
BULGA
PORTUGAL
SPAIN
ITALY
ALB
M
GREECE

CANADA

UNITED STATES
OF AMERICA

MEXICO

BERMUDA

BAHAMAS

CUBA

DOMINICAN
REPUBLIC

HAITI

CAYMAN
ISLANDS

JAMAICA
HAITI
PUERTO
RICO

VIRGIN ISLANDS
ANGUILLA
ANTIGUA
& BARBUDA
ST. KITTS
NEVIS
MONTSERRAT
GUADELOUPE (Fr)
DOMINICA
CAPE
VERDE
MARTINIQUE (Fr)
ST. LUCIA
ST. VINCENT &
GRENADINES
BARBADOS
GRENADA

GUATEMALA
BEL
EL SALVADOR
HONDURAS
NICARAGUA
COSTA RICA
PANAMA

PACIFIC
OCEAN

VENEZUELA
GUYANA
SURINAME
FRENCH
GUIANA
(Fr)
COLOMBIA
ECUADOR

PERU

TRINIDAD
& TOBAGO

BRAZIL

BOLIVIA

PARAGUAY

CHILE

URUGUAY

ARGENTINA

MOROCCO
TUNISIA
ALGERIA
LIB
WESTERN SAHARA
MAURITANIA
MALI
NIGER
SENEGAL
GAMBIA
CH
GUINEA-BISSAU
BURKINA
FASO
GUINEA
NIGERIA
SIERRA LEONE
CÔTE d'
IVOIRE
LIBERIA
TOGO
CAMEROON
EQUATORIAL GUINEA
C
GABON
CONGO
ANGO
NAMIBIA

STATES' MAIN ROLE IN GLOBAL
PROHIBITED DRUG NETWORK
1993

drug producer

drug processor

conduit for drugs and/or processor
chemicals

drug consumer

no data or insignificant

business centres for top level negotiations

states whose role in the drug network
makes them essential to the industry

major drug money laundering sites

Source: U.S. State Department.

Most states play a part in the global market for prohibited drugs, a market almost as large as those for the major permitted drugs – nicotine and alcohol.

RUSSIA

KAZAKHSTAN

MONGOLIA

UZBEKISTAN

GEO
AZER
KIRGISTAN
TURKMEN
TAJ

N KOREA
JAPAN

S KOREA

TURKEY

SYRIA
LEB
ISR
JOR
IRAQ

AFGHANISTAN

CHINA

IRAN

KUWAIT
BAHRAIN
QATAR
UAE

PAKISTAN

NEPAL
BHUTAN

PACIFIC
OCEAN

SAUDI ARABIA

OMAN

INDIA

B
DESH

TAIWAN

MYANMAR
LAOS

ERITREA
YEMEN
DJIBOUTI

THAILAND
HONG KONG

ETHIOPIA
SOMALIA

SRI LANKA

CAM
VIETNAM

PHILIPPINES

UGANDA
KENYA

BRUNEI

TANZANIA

MALAYSIA
SINGAPORE

MALAWI

MADAGASCAR

INDONESIA

PAPUA
NEW
GUINEA

MOZAMBIQUE

MAURITIUS

AUSTRALIA

CANADA

RUSSIA

KAZAKHSTAN
MONGOLIA

NEW
ZEALAND

U.S.A.

CHINA
JAPAN

ALGERIA
LIBYA
IRAN

INDIA

SUDAN

ZAIRE

INDONESIA

BRAZIL

AUSTRALIA

ANTI-DRUG ENFORCEMENT BODIES
(POLICE, CUSTOMS, JUDICIARY)
TAINTED BY DRUG MONEY *1993*

corruption at senior level

corruption at street level

no data or insignificant

Sources: U.S. State Department; press reports.

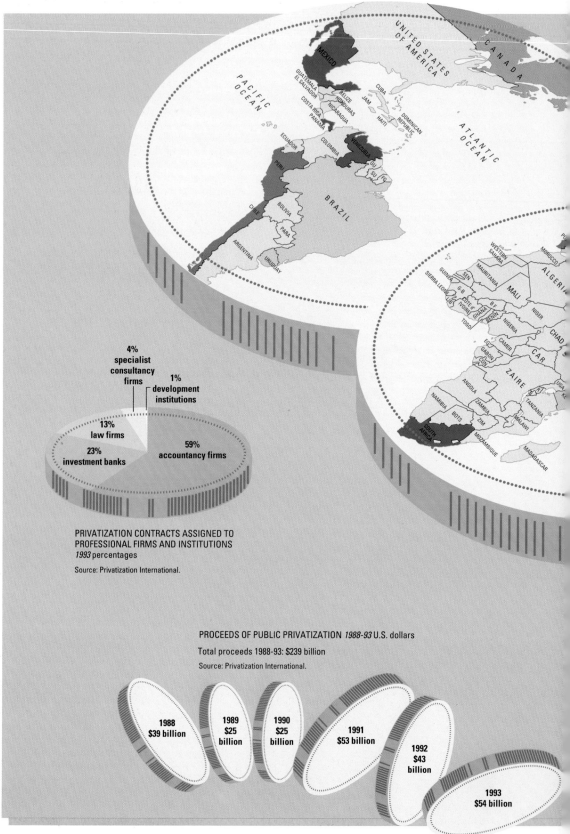

4%
**specialist
consultancy
firms**
1%
**development
institutions**

**13%
law firms**

**23%
investment banks**

**59%
accountancy firms**

**PRIVATIZATION CONTRACTS ASSIGNED TO
PROFESSIONAL FIRMS AND INSTITUTIONS**
1993 percentages

Source: Privatization International.

PROCEEDS OF PUBLIC PRIVATIZATION *1988-93* U.S. dollars

Total proceeds 1988-93: $239 billion

Source: Privatization International.

**1988
$39 billion**

**1989
$25
billion**

**1990
$25
billion**

**1991
$53 billion**

**1992
$43
billion**

**1993
$54 billion**

State assets worth a quarter of a trillion dollars (U.S. $250,000,000,000) went private publicly between 1988 and 1993. Another untold sum went private privately. The transfers continue.

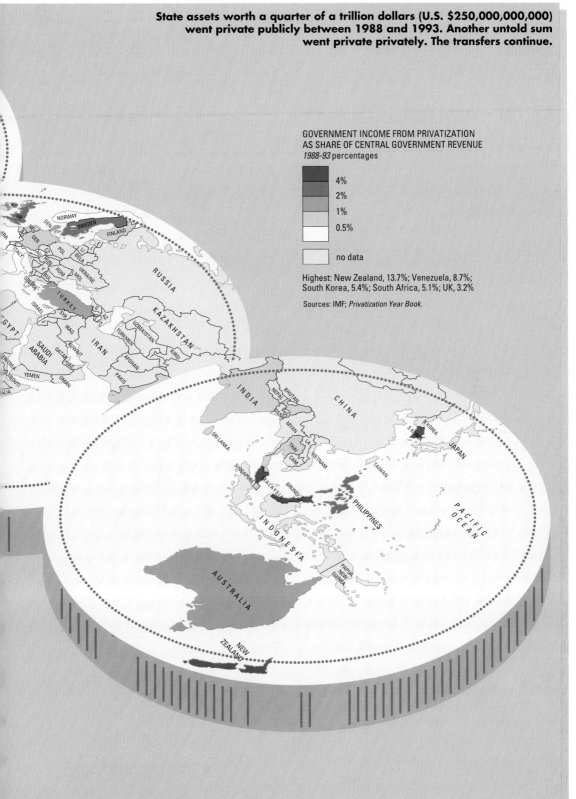

GOVERNMENT INCOME FROM PRIVATIZATION
AS SHARE OF CENTRAL GOVERNMENT REVENUE
1988-93 percentages

- 4%
- 2%
- 1%
- 0.5%

- no data

Highest: New Zealand, 13.7%; Venezuela, 8.7%;
South Korea, 5.4%; South Africa, 5.1%; UK, 3.2%

Sources: IMF; *Privatization Year Book.*

States are not equal citizens of the world of states.
Embassies in states considered important are usually
headed by a resident ambassador or equivalent. States
considered less important are more likely to be headed
by a Chargé d'Affaires or Head of Mission.

Diplomatic relations can be fairly notional: 6 of the 89
embassies in Teheran, Iran, were vacant at the end of
1992, as were 4 of the 28 in Kabul, Afghanistan. Many
missions have to share ambassadors, or be serviced by
proxies. Some are no more than post office boxes. Others
proclaim their presence but give no clue as to their
whereabouts – Namibia's mission in Yaoundé,
Cameroon, for example, or the Marshall Islands' mission
in Beijing, or Singapore's in Accra. Business in these
places cannot be brisk.

Source: *Europa*.

21 states host between 0-10 ambassadors

79 states host between 11-50 ambassadors

46 states host between 51-100 ambassadors

9 states host between 101-150 ambassadors

GREENLAND
(Den)

ICELAND

NORWAY   SWEDEN

CANADA

DENMARK

IRELAND   UNITED
KINGDOM

NETH.

BELG.   GERMANY   POLAND

CZECH   HU

AUS.

FRANCE

UNITED STATES
OF AMERICA

ITALY

PORTUGAL   SPAIN

ATLANTIC
OCEAN

MOROCCO

TUNISIA

ALGERIA   LIBY

MEXICO

BAHAMAS

WESTERN SAHARA

CUBA

DOMINICAN
REPUBLIC

CAPE VERDE

MAURITANIA

MALI

NIGER

BELIZE   JAMAICA   HAITI

GUATEMALA
EL SALVADOR

ANTIGUA & BARBUDA

SENEGAL

GAMBIA

BURKINA
FASO

CH

DOMINICA

GUINEA-BISSAU

HONDURAS

NIGERIA

NICARAGUA

GRENADA

GUINEA

BENIN

COSTA RICA

TRINIDAD & TOBAGO

SIERRA LEONE

CÔTE d'
IVOIRE

GHANA

CAM

PANAMA

VENEZUELA

GUYANA

LIBERIA

TOGO

C.

PACIFIC
OCEAN

SURINAME

EQUATORIAL
GUINEA

FRENCH GUIANA (Fr)

COLOMBIA

GABON

CONGO

Z

ECUADOR

BRAZIL

PERU

ANGOL

BOLIVIA

NAMIBIA

PARAGUAY

CHILE

URUGUAY

S

ARGENTINA

POLITICAL SYSTEMS *1993*

established multi-party,
formally democratic system

recently adopted multi-party, formally
democratic system; or in transition to one

one-party regime

military rule, in form or fact

monarchical and/or theocratic regime

disordered state: civil war or widespread
ethnic, clan or other conflict

dependent or occupied state or
assimilated territory

Sources: Keesing; *U.S. State Department Country Reports
on Human Rights Practices for 1993;* press reports.

Not all voters have equal voices. In some states, votes are simply invented or destroyed. In others, the gun, the throne or the supposed voice of God decides.

recent period of military rule

war-related or other emergency powers in use

extra-judicial violence as a form of political pressure

alleged ballot-rigging in last elections

Sources: Keesing; *U.S. State Department Country Reports on Human Rights Practices for 1993;* press reports.

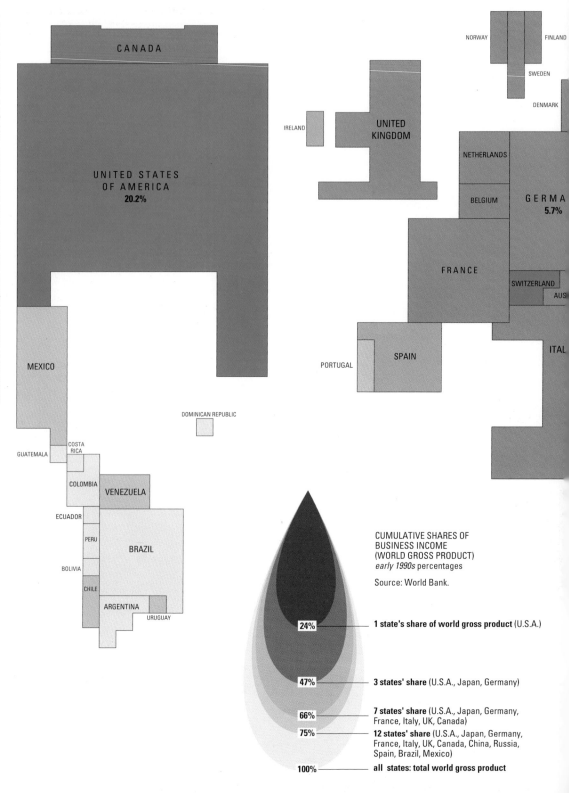

CANADA

NORWAY   FINLAND

SWEDEN

DENMARK

IRELAND

UNITED
KINGDOM

NETHERLANDS

BELGIUM

G E R M A
5.7%

UNITED STATES
OF AMERICA
20.2%

FRANCE

SWITZERLAND

AUS

MEXICO

PORTUGAL   SPAIN

ITAL

DOMINICAN REPUBLIC

COSTA
RICA

GUATEMALA

COLOMBIA

VENEZUELA

ECUADOR

PERU

BRAZIL

BOLIVIA

CHILE

ARGENTINA

URUGUAY

CUMULATIVE SHARES OF
BUSINESS INCOME
(WORLD GROSS PRODUCT)
early 1990s percentages

Source: World Bank.

24% — **1 state's share of world gross product** (U.S.A.)

47% — **3 states' share** (U.S.A., Japan, Germany)

66% — **7 states' share** (U.S.A., Japan, Germany,
France, Italy, UK, Canada)

75% — **12 states' share** (U.S.A., Japan, Germany,
France, Italy, UK, Canada, China, Russia,
Spain, Brazil, Mexico)

100% — **all states: total world gross product**

Whichever way the slippery notion of national income is measured, a handful of states invariably emerges as engrossing the lion's share.

RUSSIA

LAT

LITH

POLAND | UKRAINE

MOL

GEO

ARM | AZER

KAZAKH | KIRG

UZB

IRAN

BULGARIA | TURKEY

GREECE

PAKISTAN

JAPAN
8.6%

SOUTH KOREA

CHINA
12.4%

■ **7.8 times larger than its share of world gross product**

SYRIA

SAUDI ARABIA

ISRAEL

KUW

UAE

OMAN

YEMEN

INDIA

■ **5.5 times larger than its share of world gross product**

B'DESH

THAILAND

HONG KONG

TUN

EGYPT

GERIA

ERIA

KENYA

ZAIRE | UGAN

CAM | TANZ

ZIM

SUDAN

■ **6.1 times larger than its share of world gross product**

MOZAMBIQUE

SOUTH AFRICA

■ **8.1 times larger than its share of world gross product**

SRI LANKA

SINGAPORE | MALAYSIA

■ **6.1 times larger than its share of world gross product**

PHILIPPINES

INDONESIA

AUSTRALIA

NEW ZEALAND

PERSONAL INCOME:
STATES' SHARES OF WORLD PURCHASING POWER OR 'REAL' GROSS DOMESTIC PRODUCT
early 1990s percentages

states of 5% or over: percentage given

☐ = 1%

☐ = 0.1%

■ 5 states whose share of world purchasing power is more than 5 times their share of world gross product

PURCHASING POWER PER HEAD
early 1990s 'international' dollars

International dollars are used as a measure which attempts to gauge what states could buy if they all shopped in a single world supermarket.

20,000 'international' dollars
15,000
10,000
5,000
1,000

Sources: Heston; Population Reference Bureau.

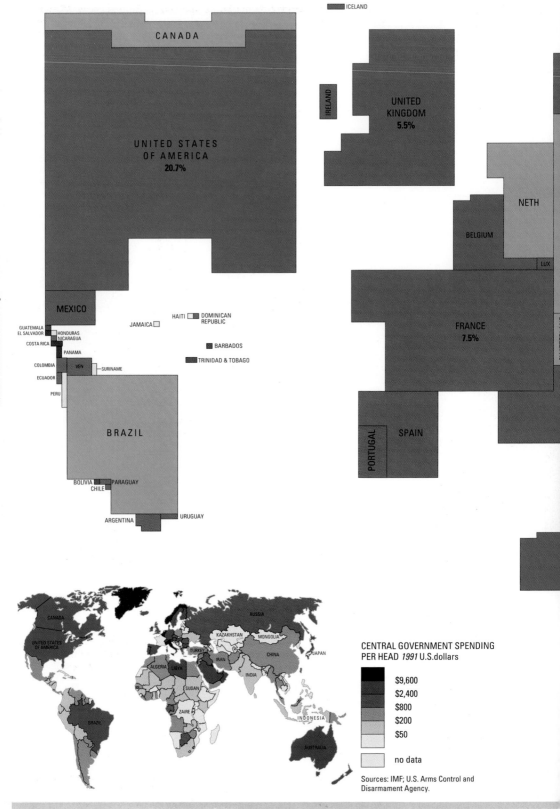

ICELAND

CANADA

IRELAND

UNITED
KINGDOM
5.5%

UNITED STATES
OF AMERICA
20.7%

NETH

BELGIUM

LUX

MEXICO

HAITI DOMINICAN
REPUBLIC

JAMAICA

GUATEMALA
EL SALVADOR HONDURAS
NICARAGUA
COSTA RICA

BARBADOS

FRANCE
7.5%

PANAMA

TRINIDAD & TOBAGO

COLOMBIA VEN SURINAME

SWITZERLAND

ECUADOR

PERU

BRAZIL

PORTUGAL

SPAIN

BOLIVIA PARAGUAY
CHILE

ARGENTINA URUGUAY

CANADA

RUSSIA

UNITED STATES
OF AMERICA

KAZAKHSTAN
MONGOLIA

TURKEY CHINA JAPAN
IRAN

ALGERIA LIBYA

INDIA

SUDAN

ZAIRE

INDONESIA

BRAZIL

AUSTRALIA

CENTRAL GOVERNMENT SPENDING
PER HEAD *1991* U.S.dollars

$9,600
$2,400
$800
$200
$50

no data

Sources: IMF; U.S. Arms Control and
Disarmament Agency.

Michael Kidron and Ronald Segal *The State of the World Atlas* 5th edition   Copyright © Myriad Editions Limited

82

In 1991, national governments spent U.S. $7 trillion — 28 percent of world income. A quarter of their spending went on paying themselves.

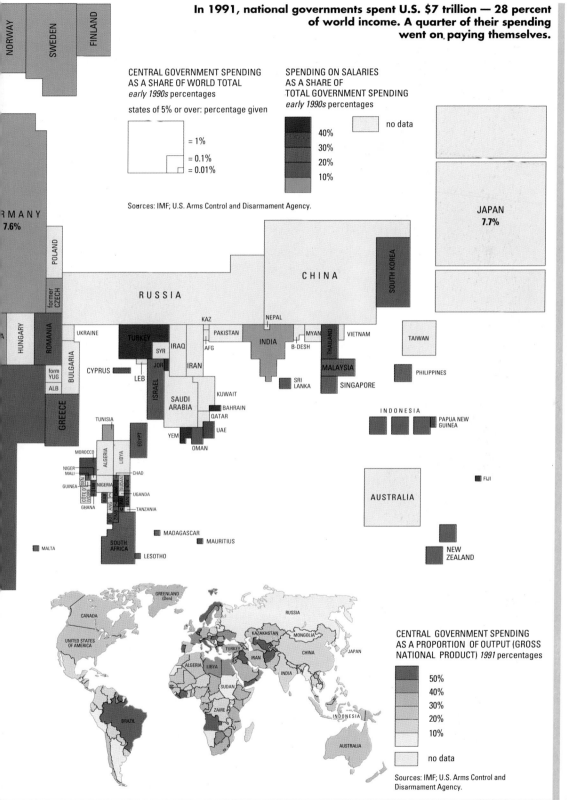

CENTRAL GOVERNMENT SPENDING
AS A SHARE OF WORLD TOTAL
early 1990s percentages

states of 5% or over: percentage given

= 1%
= 0.1%
= 0.01%

SPENDING ON SALARIES
AS A SHARE OF
TOTAL GOVERNMENT SPENDING
early 1990s percentages

no data

40%
30%
20%
10%

Sources: IMF; U.S. Arms Control and Disarmament Agency.

NORWAY
SWEDEN
FINLAND

RMANY
7.6%

JAPAN
7.7%

POLAND

former CZECH

RUSSIA

CHINA

SOUTH KOREA

HUNGARY
ROMANIA
UKRAINE
KAZ
NEPAL
PAKISTAN
PAKISTAN
MYAN
VIETNAM
TAIWAN

form YUG
BULGARIA
TURKEY
SYR
IRAQ
AFG
INDIA
B-DESH
THAILAND

ALB
CYPRUS
JOR
IRAN
MALAYSIA
PHILIPPINES

GREECE
LEB
SRI LANKA
SINGAPORE

ISRAEL
SAUDI ARABIA
KUWAIT
INDONESIA
PAPUA NEW GUINEA

TUNISIA
BAHRAIN
QATAR
UAE

EGYPT
YEM
OMAN

MOROCCO
ALGERIA
LIBYA

NIGER-MALI
CHAD
FIJI

GUINEA
NIGERIA
SUDAN
UGANDA

GHANA
TANZANIA
AUSTRALIA

MADAGASCAR
MAURITIUS

MALTA
SOUTH AFRICA
NEW ZEALAND

LESOTHO

GREENLAND (Den)

CANADA
RUSSIA

KAZAKHSTAN
MONGOLIA

UNITED STATES OF AMERICA
TURKEY
CHINA
JAPAN

ALGERIA
LIBYA
IRAN
INDIA

SUDAN

BRAZIL
ZAIRE
INDONESIA

AUSTRALIA

CENTRAL GOVERNMENT SPENDING
AS A PROPORTION OF OUTPUT (GROSS
NATIONAL PRODUCT) *1991* percentages

50%
40%
30%
20%
10%

no data

Sources: IMF; U.S. Arms Control and
Disarmament Agency.

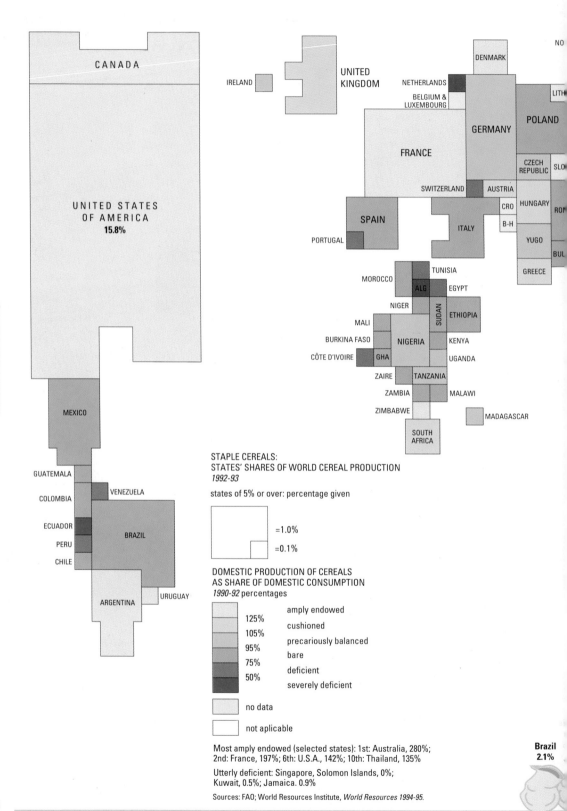

Michael Kidron and Ronald Segal *The State of the World Atlas* 5th edition   Copyright © Myriad Editions Limited

CANADA

IRELAND

UNITED
KINGDOM

DENMARK

NO

NETHERLANDS

BELGIUM &
LUXEMBOURG

LITH

POLAND

GERMANY

FRANCE

CZECH
REPUBLIC

SLO

UNITED STATES
OF AMERICA
15.8%

SWITZERLAND

AUSTRIA

CRO

HUNGARY

RO

SPAIN

ITALY

B-H

YUGO

PORTUGAL

BUL

GREECE

TUNISIA

MOROCCO

ALG

EGYPT

NIGER

SUDAN

ETHIOPIA

MALI

MEXICO

BURKINA FASO

NIGERIA

KENYA

CÔTE D'IVOIRE

GHA

UGANDA

ZAIRE

TANZANIA

GUATEMALA

ZAMBIA

MALAWI

VENEZUELA

ZIMBABWE

MADAGASCAR

COLOMBIA

ECUADOR

BRAZIL

SOUTH
AFRICA

PERU

CHILE

ARGENTINA

URUGUAY

STAPLE CEREALS:
STATES' SHARES OF WORLD CEREAL PRODUCTION
1992-93

states of 5% or over: percentage given

	=1.0%
	=0.1%

DOMESTIC PRODUCTION OF CEREALS
AS SHARE OF DOMESTIC CONSUMPTION
1990-92 percentages

	125%	amply endowed
	105%	cushioned
	95%	precariously balanced
	75%	bare
	50%	deficient
		severely deficient

no data

not aplicable

Most amply endowed (selected states): 1st: Australia, 280%;
2nd: France, 197%; 6th: U.S.A., 142%; 10th: Thailand, 135%

Utterly deficient: Singapore, Solomon Islands, 0%;
Kuwait, 0.5%; Jamaica. 0.9%

Sources: FAO; World Resources Institute, *World Resources 1994-95*.

**Brazil
2.1%**

84

A state that cannot guarantee its citizens adequate food is a state in crisis.

DEN

FINLAND

RUSSIA
5.1%

UKRAINE

MOOVA

KAZAKHSTAN

AZER | UZB | KIRG

AFGHANISTAN

TURKEY

IRAQ

IRAN

PAKISTAN

SYRIA

SAUDI ARABIA

CHINA
21%

NORTH KOREA

SOUTH KOREA

JAPAN

NEPAL

BANGLADESH

MYANMAR

THAILAND

CAM

LAOS

VIETNAM

PHILIPPINES

INDIA
10.4%

MALAYSIA

ALL OTHER STATES

INDONESIA

AUSTRALIA

SRI LANKA

TOP EXPORTERS OF CEREALS
net percentages of world share *1990-92*

Source: World Resources Institute,
World Resources 1994-95.

Hungary 0.8%
Sweden 0.6%
rest of world

Denmark 1.3%
UK 1.9%
Thailand
Argentina
5%
3%
4.1%

TOP IMPORTERS OF CEREALS
(EXCLUDING FORMER USSR)
net percentages of world share *1990-92*

Source: World Resources Institute,
World Resources 1994-95.

Japan
14.6%

China
8%

South Korea
5.4%

Australia
7.5%

Canada
11.6%

U.S.A.
49.1%

France
15.1%

ia,

Mexico
3.6%

Egypt
4.4%

CANADA

☐ ICELAND

NORWAY | SWEDEN | FINLAND

IRELAND

UNITED
KINGDOM

DENMARK

UNITED STATES
OF AMERICA
22.4%

NETH

BELGIUM

GERMANY
11.1%

LUX

POL

FRANCE
5.3%

MEXICO

☐ CUBA   ☐ DOMINICAN
REPUBLIC

SPAIN

GUATEMALA
EL SAL
HONDURAS
NICARAGUA   PANAMA
COSTA RICA   COL
ECUADOR
PERU

JAMAICA ☐

☐ TRINIDAD & TOBAGO

VENEZUELA

PORTUGAL

ITALY

BOLIVIA
PARAGUAY

BRAZIL

CHILE

☐ MALTA

URUGUAY

ARGENTINA

STATES' SHARES OF WORLD
MANUFACTURING BY VALUE OF OUTPUT
1990 or latest available date

states of 5% or over: percentage given

☐ = 1%
☐ = 0.1%
▫ = 0.01%

RISE OR FALL
IN STATES' SHARES
1980-90 percentages

rise

100% rise
75%
50%
25%

fall

up to 25% fall

no data

Highest rises: South Korea, 232%
Malaysia, 149%
Furthest falls: Peru, -24%; Poland, -16%; Uruguay, -12%

Source: UN Industrial Development Organization.

The U.S.A. and Japan together account for over 40 percent of the world's total manufacturing output. Some states are rapidly growing industrial powers. Others are shrinking fast.

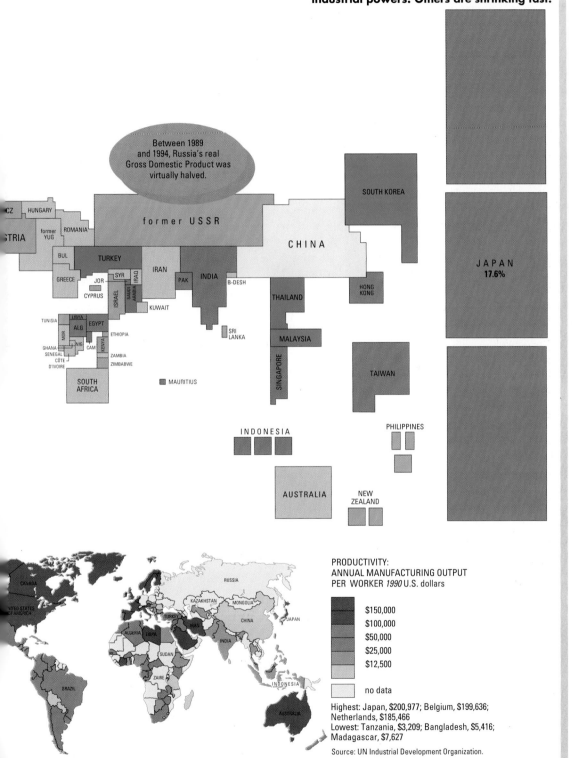

Between 1989 and 1994, Russia's real Gross Domestic Product was virtually halved.

CZ
HUNGARY
former YUG
STRIA
ROMANIA
former USSR
SOUTH KOREA
BUL
TURKEY
IRAN
CHINA
GREECE
JOR
SYR
IRAQ
PAK
INDIA
B-DESH
SAUDI ARABIA
ISRAEL
CYPRUS
KUWAIT
HONG KONG
TUNISIA
LIBYA
EGYPT
THAILAND
ALG
MOR
NIG
ETHIOPIA
SRI LANKA
MALAYSIA
GHANA
CAM
KENYA
SENEGAL
CÔTE D'IVOIRE
ZAMBIA
ZIMBABWE
SINGAPORE
TAIWAN
SOUTH AFRICA
MAURITIUS

JAPAN
17.6%

INDONESIA
PHILIPPINES

AUSTRALIA
NEW ZEALAND

PRODUCTIVITY:
ANNUAL MANUFACTURING OUTPUT
PER WORKER *1990* U.S. dollars

CANADA
RUSSIA
KAZAKHSTAN
MONGOLIA
UNITED STATES OF AMERICA
TURKEY
CHINA
JAPAN
ALGERIA
LIBYA
IRAN
INDIA
SUDAN
ZAIRE
INDONESIA
BRAZIL
AUSTRALIA

$150,000
$100,000
$50,000
$25,000
$12,500

no data

Highest: Japan, $200,977; Belgium, $199,636;
Netherlands, $185,466
Lowest: Tanzania, $3,209; Bangladesh, $5,416;
Madagascar, $7,627

Source: UN Industrial Development Organization.

CANADA

UNITED STATES
OF AMERICA
12.0%

MEXICO

COLOMBIA

VENEZUELA

BRAZIL

CHILE

ARGENTINA

IRELAND

UNITED
KINGDOM
5.1%

NORWAY

SWEDEN

FINLAND

DENMARK

NETHERLANDS

GERMANY
11.5%

BELGIUM &
LUXEMBURG

FRANCE
6.3%

SWITZERLAND

PORTUGAL

SPAIN

ITALY

MOROCCO

ALGERIA

TUNISIA

LIBYA

NIGERIA

SOUTH
AFRICA

ALL OTHER STATES

STATES' SHARES OF WORLD TRADE
IN EXPORTED GOODS
1992 percentages

states of 5% or over: percentage given

=1.0%

=0.1%

RISE OR FALL
IN STATES' SHARES
1982 -92

rise

over two-thirds

one-third to two-thirds

up to one third

no change

fall

up to one third

one third to two-thirds

over two-thirds

not applicable

Highest rises: Hong Kong, 186%; Thailand, 135%; Portugal, 123%
Furthest falls: Kuwait, Saudi Arabia, 69%; Libya, 66%

Source: GATT.

Three states - Germany, Japan and the U.S.A. - account for virtually a third of all trade in exported goods.

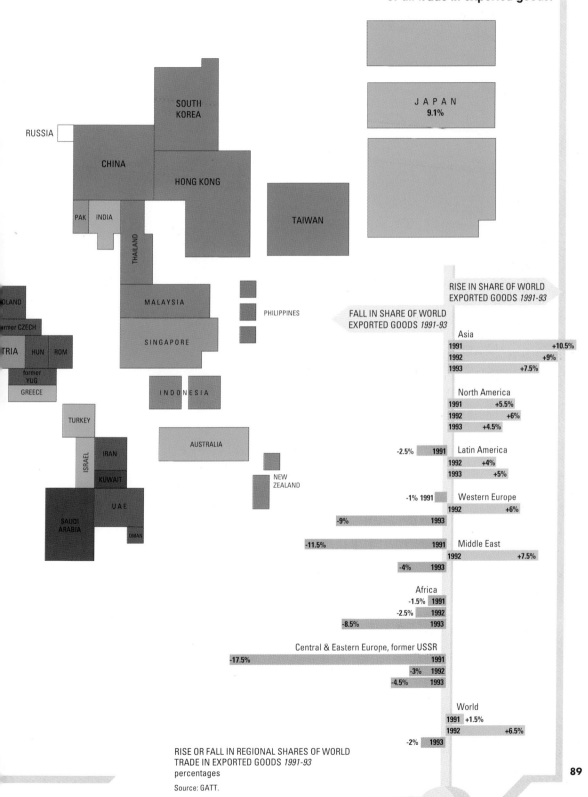

SOUTH KOREA

RUSSIA

CHINA

HONG KONG

PAK INDIA

THAILAND

TAIWAN

JAPAN
9.1%

POLAND

former CZECH

TRIA HUN ROM

former YUG

GREECE

MALAYSIA

SINGAPORE

PHILIPPINES

RISE IN SHARE OF WORLD
EXPORTED GOODS *1991-93*

FALL IN SHARE OF WORLD
EXPORTED GOODS *1991-93*

Asia

1991	+10.5%
1992	+9%
1993	+7.5%

INDONESIA

TURKEY

North America

1991	+5.5%
1992	+6%
1993	+4.5%

AUSTRALIA

ISRAEL IRAN

KUWAIT

NEW ZEALAND

Latin America

-2.5%	1991
1992	+4%
1993	+5%

SAUDI ARABIA UAE

OMAN

Western Europe

-1%	1991
1992	+6%
-9%	1993

Middle East

-11.5%	1991
1992	+7.5%
-4%	1993

Africa

-1.5%	1991
-2.5%	1992
-8.5%	1993

Central & Eastern Europe, former USSR

-17.5%	1991
-3%	1992
-4.5%	1993

World

1991	+1.5%
1992	+6.5%
-2%	1993

RISE OR FALL IN REGIONAL SHARES OF WORLD
TRADE IN EXPORTED GOODS *1991-93*
percentages
Source: GATT.

CANADA

UNITED STATES
OF AMERICA
16.2%

IRELAND

UNITED
KINGDOM
5.5%

MEXICO

JAMAICA

NETHERLANDS
ANTILLES

BAHAMAS

COLOMBIA

VENEZUELA

DOMINICAN
REPUBLIC

FRANCE
10.2%

BRAZIL

CHILE

ARGENTINA

PORTUGAL

SPAIN

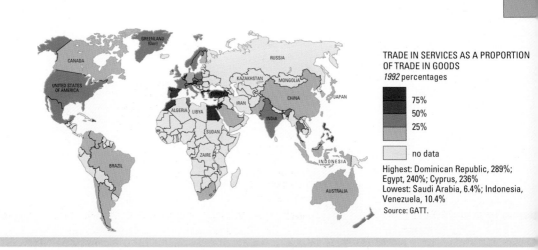

TRADE IN SERVICES AS A PROPORTION
OF TRADE IN GOODS
1992 percentages

- 75%
- 50%
- 25%
- no data

Highest: Dominican Republic, 289%;
Egypt, 240%; Cyprus, 236%
Lowest: Saudi Arabia, 6.4%; Indonesia,
Venezuela, 10.4%
Source: GATT.

Two states account for over a quarter, six states for nearly half, of all exports in commercial services.

NORWAY
SWEDEN
FINLAND
NETHERLANDS
DENMARK
POLAND
CZECH REP & SLOVAKIA
GERMANY 6.4%
BELGIUM & LUXEMBOURG
HUNGARY
AUSTRIA
ITALY 6.5%
former YUG
GREECE
CYPRUS
TURKEY
TUN
EGYPT
ISRAEL
JOR
KUWAIT
MOR
SAUDI ARABIA
SOUTH AFRICA

JAPAN 5%
SOUTH KOREA
CHINA
HONG KONG
PAK
INDIA
THAILAND
TAIWAN
MALAYSIA
SINGAPORE
PHILIPPINES
INDONESIA
AUSTRALIA
NEW ZEALAND

STATES' SHARES OF WORLD TRADE IN COMMERCIAL SERVICES *1992*

states of 5% or over: percentage given

□ = 1%
□ = 0.1%

RISE OR FALL IN STATES' SHARES
1982-92 percentages

rise

over two-thirds
one third to two-thirds
up to one third
no change

fall

up to one third
one third to two-thirds
over two-thirds

Highest rises: Indonesia, 150%; Hungary, 100%
Furthest fall: Saudi Arabia, 74%

Source: GATT.

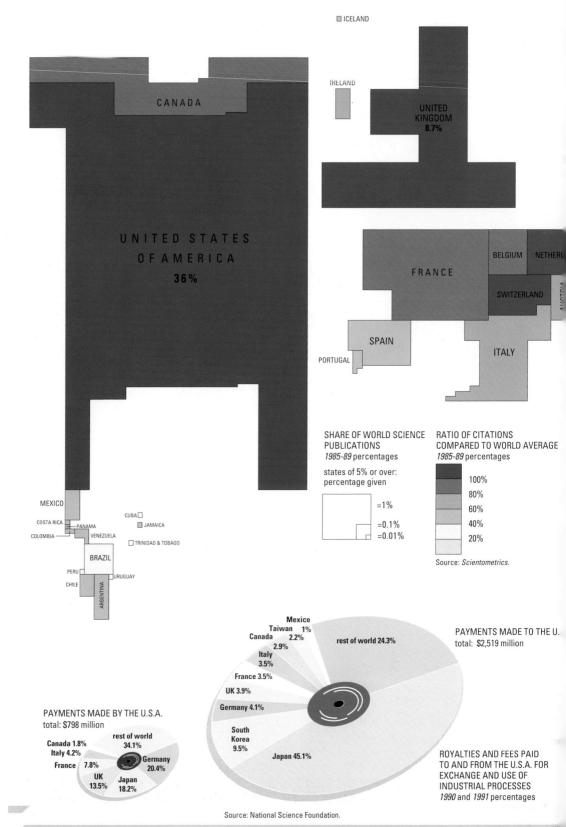

ICELAND

CANADA

IRELAND

UNITED
KINGDOM
8.7%

UNITED STATES
OF AMERICA

36%

BELGIUM   NETHERL

FRANCE

SWITZERLAND

SPAIN

PORTUGAL

ITALY

MEXICO

COSTA RICA

PANAMA

COLOMBIA

VENEZUELA

CUBA

JAMAICA

TRINIDAD & TOBAGO

BRAZIL

PERU

CHILE

URUGUAY

ARGENTINA

SHARE OF WORLD SCIENCE
PUBLICATIONS
1985-89 percentages

states of 5% or over:
percentage given

= 1%

= 0.1%

= 0.01%

RATIO OF CITATIONS
COMPARED TO WORLD AVERAGE
1985-89 percentages

100%
80%
60%
40%
20%

Source: *Scientometrics.*

Mexico 1%
Taiwan
2.2%
Canada
2.9%
Italy
3.5%
France 3.5%
UK 3.9%
Germany 4.1%
South
Korea
9.5%
Japan 45.1%

rest of world 24.3%

PAYMENTS MADE TO THE U.
total: $2,519 million

PAYMENTS MADE BY THE U.S.A.
total: $798 million

Canada 1.8%
Italy 4.2%
France 7.8%
UK
13.5%
Japan
18.2%
Germany
20.4%
rest of world
34.1%

ROYALTIES AND FEES PAID
TO AND FROM THE U.S.A. FOR
EXCHANGE AND USE OF
INDUSTRIAL PROCESSES
1990 and *1991* percentages

Source: National Science Foundation.

The U.S.A. is the super science power — the biggest and most effective science producer and by far the biggest science market.

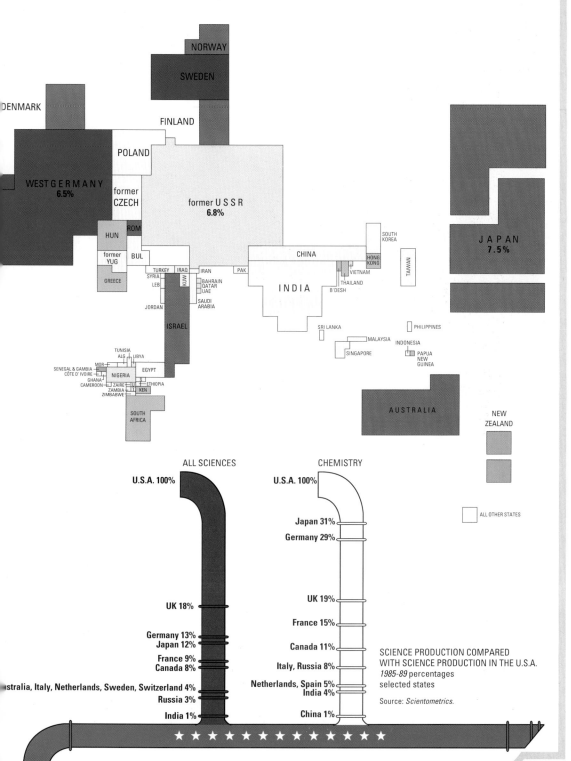

NORWAY

SWEDEN

DENMARK

FINLAND

POLAND

WEST GERMANY
6.5%

former
CZECH

HUN

ROM

former
YUG

BUL

GREECE

former U S S R
6.8%

SOUTH
KOREA

CHINA

HONG
KONG

TAIWAN

JAPAN
7.5%

TURKEY IRAQ IRAN PAK

SYRIA

LEB

KUW

BAHRAIN
QATAR
UAE

VIETNAM

THAILAND

B'DESH

JORDAN

SAUDI
ARABIA

I N D I A

ISRAEL

SRI LANKA

PHILIPPINES

TUNISIA

ALG LIBYA

MOR

SENEGAL & GAMBIA
CÔTE D' IVOIRE

GHANA

CAMEROON

NIGERIA

EGYPT

S
U
D ZAIRE

ZAMBIA

ZIMBABWE

KEN

ETHIOPIA

MALAYSIA

SINGAPORE

INDONESIA

PAPUA
NEW
GUINEA

SOUTH
AFRICA

AUSTRALIA

NEW
ZEALAND

ALL OTHER STATES

ALL SCIENCES

U.S.A. 100%

UK 18%

Germany 13%
Japan 12%

France 9%
Canada 8%

Australia, Italy, Netherlands, Sweden, Switzerland 4%

Russia 3%

India 1%

CHEMISTRY

U.S.A. 100%

Japan 31%
Germany 29%

UK 19%

France 15%

Canada 11%

Italy, Russia 8%

Netherlands, Spain 5%
India 4%

China 1%

SCIENCE PRODUCTION COMPARED
WITH SCIENCE PRODUCTION IN THE U.S.A.
1985-89 percentages
selected states

Source: *Scientometrics.*

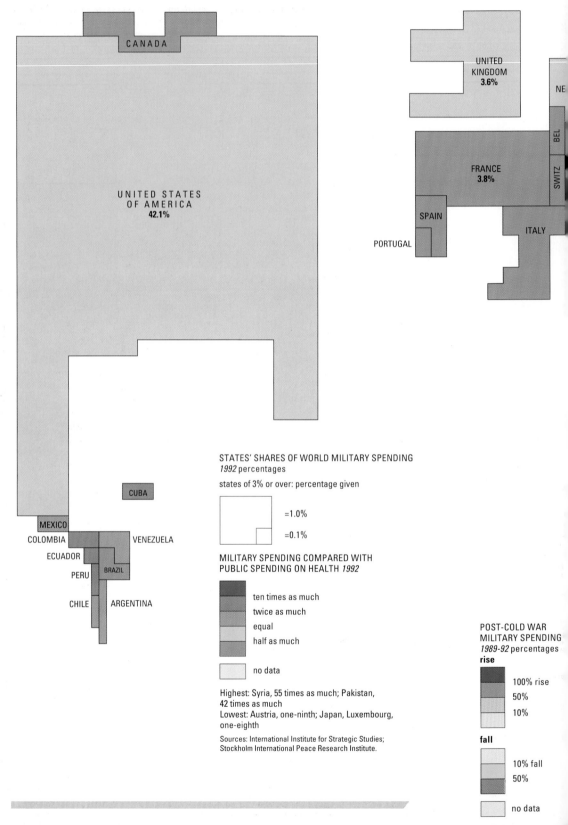

CANADA

UNITED STATES
OF AMERICA
42.1%

UNITED
KINGDOM
3.6%

NE

BEL

FRANCE
3.8%

SWITZ

SPAIN

PORTUGAL

ITALY

CUBA

MEXICO

COLOMBIA

VENEZUELA

ECUADOR

PERU

BRAZIL

CHILE

ARGENTINA

STATES' SHARES OF WORLD MILITARY SPENDING
1992 percentages

states of 3% or over: percentage given

=1.0%

=0.1%

MILITARY SPENDING COMPARED WITH
PUBLIC SPENDING ON HEALTH *1992*

ten times as much

twice as much

equal

half as much

no data

Highest: Syria, 55 times as much; Pakistan,
42 times as much
Lowest: Austria, one-ninth; Japan, Luxembourg,
one-eighth

Sources: International Institute for Strategic Studies;
Stockholm International Peace Research Institute.

POST-COLD WAR
MILITARY SPENDING
1989-92 percentages
rise

100% rise

50%

10%

fall

10% fall

50%

no data

The military take U.S. $600 billion a year, a million dollars a minute and more than three-quarters as much as public spending on health.

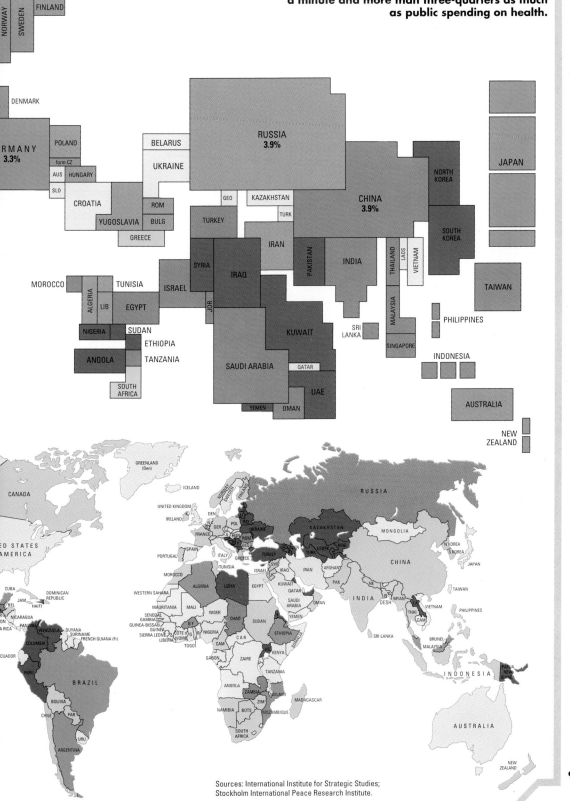

Sources: International Institute for Strategic Studies; Stockholm International Peace Research Institute.

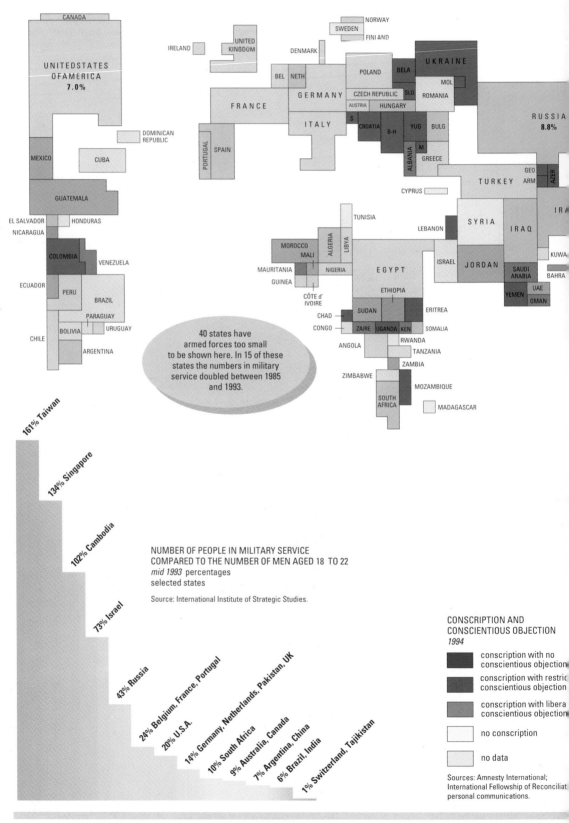

CANADA

UNITED STATES
OF AMERICA
7.0%

IRELAND

UNITED
KINGDOM

NORWAY

SWEDEN

FINLAND

DENMARK

BEL NETH

GERMANY

POLAND

BELA

UKRAINE

MOL

CZECH REPUBLIC

SLO

ROMANIA

AUSTRIA HUNGARY

FRANCE

ITALY

S

CROATIA

B-H

YUG

BULG

ALBANIA

M

GREECE

GEO

ARM

AZER

RUSSIA
8.8%

TURKEY

IRA

DOMINICAN
REPUBLIC

MEXICO

CUBA

PORTUGAL

SPAIN

CYPRUS

GUATEMALA

EL SALVADOR   HONDURAS

NICARAGUA

COLOMBIA

VENEZUELA

ECUADOR

PERU

BRAZIL

PARAGUAY

BOLIVIA   URUGUAY

CHILE

ARGENTINA

TUNISIA

LEBANON

SYRIA

IRAQ

MOROCCO

MALI

ALGERIA

LIBYA

ISRAEL

JORDAN

SAUDI
ARABIA

KUWA

BAHRA

MAURITANIA

NIGERIA

EGYPT

GUINEA

CÔTE d'
IVOIRE

ETHIOPIA

YEMEN

UAE

OMAN

CHAD

SUDAN

ERITREA

CONGO

ZAIRE

UGANDA

KEN

SOMALIA

RWANDA

ANGOLA

TANZANIA

ZAMBIA

ZIMBABWE

MOZAMBIQUE

SOUTH
AFRICA

MADAGASCAR

40 states have
armed forces too small
to be shown here. In 15 of these
states the numbers in military
service doubled between 1985
and 1993.

161% Taiwan

134% Singapore

102% Cambodia

73% Israel

43% Russia

24% Belgium, France, Portugal

20% U.S.A.

14% Germany, Netherlands, Pakistan, UK

10% South Africa

9% Australia, Canada

7% Argentina, China

6% Brazil, India

1% Switzerland, Tajikistan

NUMBER OF PEOPLE IN MILITARY SERVICE
COMPARED TO THE NUMBER OF MEN AGED 18 TO 22
mid 1993 percentages
selected states

Source: International Institute of Strategic Studies.

CONSCRIPTION AND
CONSCIENTIOUS OBJECTION
1994

conscription with no
conscientious objection

conscription with restric
conscientious objection

conscription with libera
conscientious objection

no conscription

no data

Sources: Amnesty International;
International Fellowship of Reconciliat
personal communications.

96

30 million people are under arms fulltime in the world - more than 10 percent of the number of men aged 18 to 22.

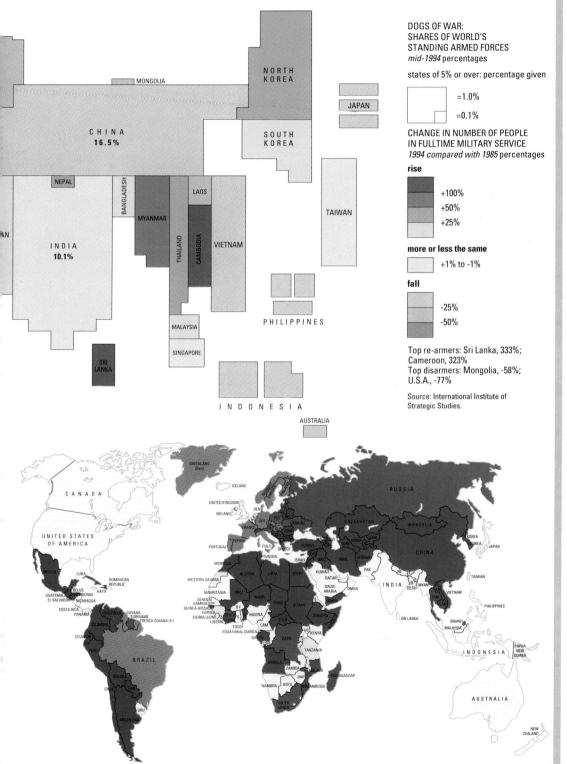

MONGOLIA

NORTH KOREA

JAPAN

CHINA
16.5%

SOUTH KOREA

NEPAL

BANGLADESH

LAOS

TAIWAN

MYANMAR

THAILAND

CAMBODIA

VIETNAM

INDIA
10.1%

MALAYSIA

SINGAPORE

PHILIPPINES

SRI LANKA

INDONESIA

AUSTRALIA

DOGS OF WAR:
SHARES OF WORLD'S
STANDING ARMED FORCES
mid-1994 percentages

states of 5% or over: percentage given

☐ =1.0%

☐ =0.1%

CHANGE IN NUMBER OF PEOPLE
IN FULLTIME MILITARY SERVICE
1994 compared with 1985 percentages

rise

+100%

+50%

+25%

more or less the same

+1% to -1%

fall

-25%

-50%

Top re-armers: Sri Lanka, 333%;
Cameroon, 323%
Top disarmers: Mongolia, -58%;
U.S.A., -77%

Source: International Institute of
Strategic Studies.

97

GREENLAND
(Den)

ICELAND

CANADA

NORWAY

SWEDEN

UNITED
KINGDOM

DENMARK

IRELAND

NETH
BEL
GERMANY

POLA

CZECH

AUS

FRANCE

ITALY

PORTUGAL

SPAIN

12 states   38 states

UNITED STATES
OF AMERICA

MOROCCO

TUNISIA

ALGERIA

LIB

WESTERN SAHARA

MEXICO

ATLANTIC
OCEAN

MAURITANIA

MALI

NIGER

SENEGAL

CUBA

GAMBIA

GUINEA-BISSAU

BURKINA
FASO

BELIZE
HONDURAS

DOMINICAN
REPUBLIC

JAMAICA

HAITI

GUINEA

CÔTE d'
IVOIRE

BENIN

NIGERIA

GUATEMALA
EL SALVADOR

SIERRA LEONE

GHANA

NICARAGUA

COSTA RICA

PANAMA

TRINIDAD & TOBAGO

VENEZUELA

GUYANA

SURINAME

FRENCH GUIANA (Fr)

LIBERIA

TOGO

CAMEROON

EQUATORIAL GUINEA

GABON

PACIFIC
OCEAN

COLOMBIA

CONGO

ECUADOR

ANGO

BRAZIL

PERU

NAMIB

BOLIVIA

LICENSED KILLING:
LEGAL STATUS OF CAPITAL PUNISHMENT
early 1990s

PARAGUAY

CHILE

URUGUAY

ARGENTINA

abolished for all crimes

abolished for ordinary crimes but retained
for crimes against the state and its agents,
or for crimes committed in extraordinary
times, such as war

retained for ordinary crimes but
no executions since 1980 or independence

retained and used for ordinary crimes

federal system: status varies

UNLICENSED KILLING

extra-judicial killing and/or officially-inspired
'disappearances' reported to Amnesty International

Sources: Amnesty International; U.S. State Department.

Michael Kidron and Ronald Segal *The State of the World Atlas* 5th edition   Copyright © Myriad Editions Limited

**States deal harshly with their citizens.
Many terrorize them.**

RUSSIA

KAZAKHSTAN

MONGOLIA

NE

GEO
AZER
TURKEY
SYRIA
LEB
JOR
IRAQ
KUWAIT
IRAN
BAHRAIN
QATAR
UAE
SAUDI ARABIA
OMAN
ERITREA
YEMEN
DJIBOUTI
ETHIOPIA
SOMALIA
UGANDA
KENYA

UZBEKISTAN
KIRGISTAN
TURKMEN
TAJ.
AFGHANISTAN
PAKISTAN

CHINA

N.KOREA   JAPAN
S.KOREA

NEPAL   BHUTAN
INDIA   B'DESH
MYANMAR   LAOS
THAILAND   VIETNAM
CAM

TAIWAN
HONG KONG

PACIFIC
OCEAN

PHILIPPINES

MALDIVES   SRI LANKA

BRUNEI

MALAYSIA
SINGAPORE

INDONESIA   PAPUA
NEW
GUINEA

TANZANIA
COMOROS
MALAWI
MADAGASCAR
MAURITIUS
MOZAMBIQUE

AUSTRALIA

FIJI   COOK ISLANDS

NEW
ZEALAND

CANADA
U.S.A.
RUSSIA
KAZAKHSTAN   MONGOLIA
TURKEY   CHINA
ALGERIA   LIBYA   IRAN
SUDAN   INDIA
BRAZIL   ZAIRE
INDONESIA
AUSTRALIA

**TORTURE BY STATE EMPLOYEES
(POLICE, THE MILITARY OR PRISON OFFICERS)**
1991-93

one or more case of torture
reported to Amnesty International

other states or no data

Source: Amnesty International.

99

NORWAY
SWEDEN
FINLAN
ESTON
LATVI
DENMARK
LITHUANIA
IRELAND
BELA
UNITED
KINGDOM
NETH
POLAND
UKRA
BEL
GERMANY
CZECH
REPUBLIC
SLOVAK
FRANCE
SWITZ
AUSTRIA
HUNGARY
ROMA
SLO
CROATIA
B·H
YUG
BULG
PORTUGAL
SPAIN
ITALY
ALB
M
GREECE

CANADA

UNITED STATES
OF AMERICA

MEXICO

CUBA
DOMINICAN
REPUBLIC
BELIZE
JAMAICA
HAITI
GUATEMALA
HONDURAS
EL SALVADOR
NICARAGUA
COSTA RICA
PANAMA

☐ BARBADOS

TRINIDAD & TOBAGO

VENEZUELA
GUYANA
SURINAME
FRENCH GUIANA (Fr)
COLOMBIA

ECUADOR

ATLANTIC
OCEAN

MOROCCO
TUNISIA
ALGERIA
LIB
WESTERN SAHARA
MAURITANIA
MALI
NIGER
SENEGAL
GAMBIA
GUINEA-BISSAU
BURKINA
FASO
CH
GUINEA
NIGERIA
SIERRA LEONE
CÔTE d'
IVOIRE
GHANA
BENIN
C
LIBERIA
TOGO
CAMEROON
EQUATORIAL GUINEA
GABON
CONGO

ANGO

NAMIBI

PERU

BOLIVIA

CHILE

BRAZIL

PARAGUAY

URUGUAY

ARGENTINA

TOP TEN EXPORTERS
OF MAJOR CONVENTIONAL ARMS
1992 U.S. dollars at *1990* prices
Source: SIPRI.

France 6.3%
UK 5.2%
former
Czechoslovakia 4.2%
Italy 1.8%
Netherlands 1.7%
Sweden 0.6%
rest of world 4.5%

China
8.3%

Germany
10.5%

Russia
11.1%

U.S.A.
45.8%

TOP TEN IMPORTERS
OF MAJOR CONVENTIONAL ARMS
1992 percentages of world total
Source: SIPRI.

Greece 10.4%
Turkey 8.2%
India 6.5%
Japan 5.9%
Saudi Arabia 4.8%
Iran 4.8%
Pakistan 2.3%
S. Korea 2.2%
Spain 2.0%
Germany 0.8%

During 1994 more than 35 states were waging war inside or outside their territories. Altogether more than 50 states were at war at some time between 1990 and 1994.

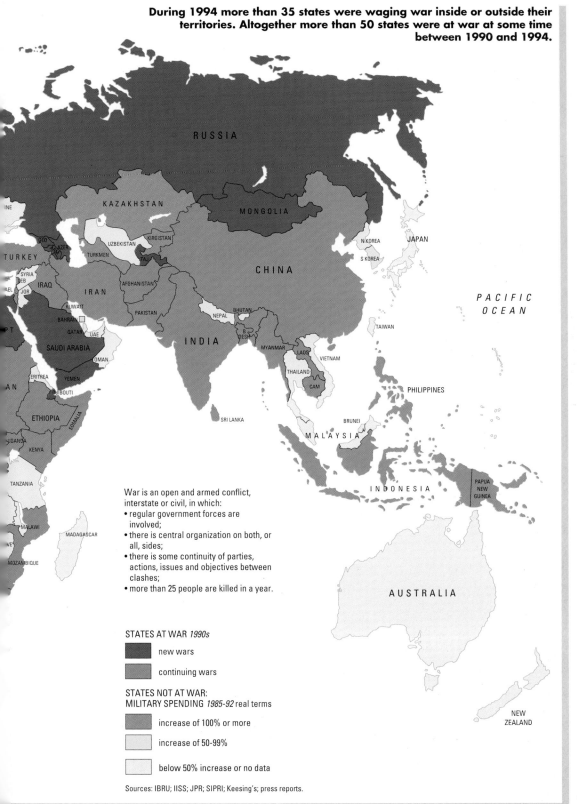

RUSSIA

KAZAKHSTAN

MONGOLIA

INE

GEO
AZER
TURKEY
UZBEKISTAN
KIRGISTAN
TURKMEN
TAJ
N.KOREA   JAPAN
S.KOREA

SYRIA
LEB
IRAQ
IRAN
AFGHANISTAN
CHINA

AEL
JOR
KUWAIT
PAKISTAN
NEPAL   BHUTAN
TAIWAN

PACIFIC OCEAN

T
BAHRAIN
QATAR   UAE
SAUDI ARABIA
OMAN
INDIA
B.DESH
MYANMAR
LAOS   VIETNAM

ERITREA
YEMEN
DJIBOUTI
THAILAND
CAM

AN
ETHIOPIA
SOMALIA
PHILIPPINES

UGANDA
KENYA
SRI LANKA
BRUNEI

TANZANIA
MALAYSIA

War is an open and armed conflict,
interstate or civil, in which:
• regular government forces are
  involved;
• there is central organization on both, or
  all, sides;
• there is some continuity of parties,
  actions, issues and objectives between
  clashes;
• more than 25 people are killed in a year.

INDONESIA
PAPUA NEW GUINEA

MALAWI
MADAGASCAR

VE
MOZAMBIQUE

AUSTRALIA

STATES AT WAR *1990s*

new wars

continuing wars

STATES NOT AT WAR:
MILITARY SPENDING *1985-92* real terms

increase of 100% or more

increase of 50-99%

below 50% increase or no data

NEW ZEALAND

Sources: IBRU; IISS; JPR; SIPRI; Keesing's; press reports.

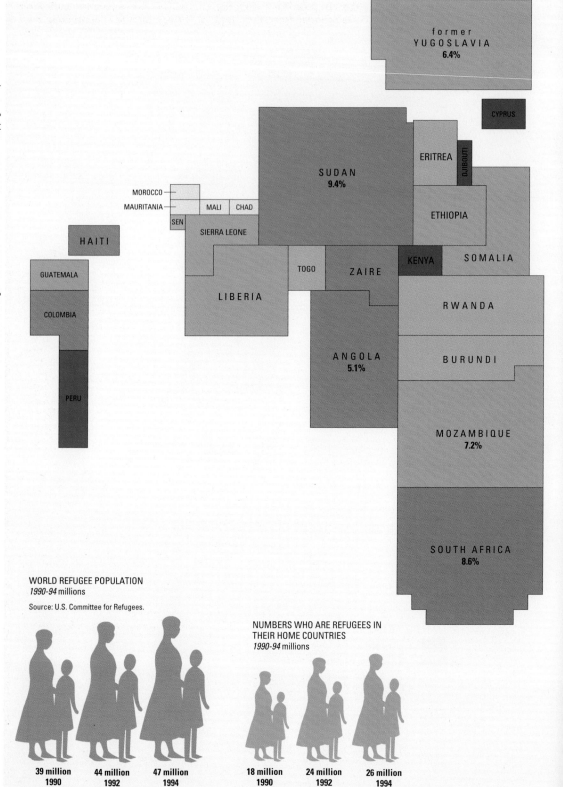

former
YUGOSLAVIA
6.4%

CYPRUS

ERITREA

DJIBOUTI

SUDAN
9.4%

MOROCCO
MAURITANIA

MALI   CHAD

SEN

SIERRA LEONE

ETHIOPIA

HAITI

GUATEMALA

COLOMBIA

PERU

TOGO

ZAIRE

KENYA

SOMALIA

LIBERIA

RWANDA

ANGOLA
5.1%

BURUNDI

MOZAMBIQUE
7.2%

SOUTH AFRICA
8.6%

WORLD REFUGEE POPULATION
1990-94 millions

Source: U.S. Committee for Refugees.

NUMBERS WHO ARE REFUGEES IN
THEIR HOME COUNTRIES
1990-94 millions

39 million
1990

44 million
1992

47 million
1994

18 million
1990

24 million
1992

26 million
1994

At least 47 million people have abandoned their homes in fear for their lives and livelihoods. More than half are refugees in their own countries.

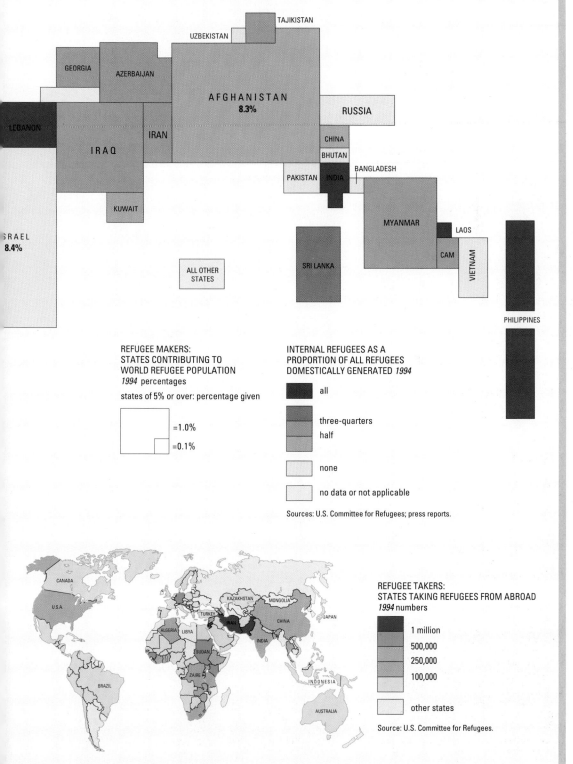

TAJIKISTAN

UZBEKISTAN

GEORGIA

AZERBAIJAN

AFGHANISTAN
8.3%

RUSSIA

LEBANON

IRAN

CHINA

IRAQ

BHUTAN

BANGLADESH

PAKISTAN   INDIA

KUWAIT

MYANMAR   LAOS

ISRAEL
8.4%

CAM

VIETNAM

ALL OTHER
STATES

SRI LANKA

PHILIPPINES

REFUGEE MAKERS:
STATES CONTRIBUTING TO
WORLD REFUGEE POPULATION
1994 percentages

states of 5% or over: percentage given

=1.0%

=0.1%

INTERNAL REFUGEES AS A
PROPORTION OF ALL REFUGEES
DOMESTICALLY GENERATED *1994*

all

three-quarters

half

no data or not applicable

Sources: U.S. Committee for Refugees; press reports.

CANADA

U.S.A.

KAZAKHSTAN   MONGOLIA

TURKEY   IRAN   JAPAN

ALGERIA LIBYA   CHINA

SUDAN   INDIA

ZAIRE   INDONESIA

BRAZIL

AUSTRALIA

REFUGEE TAKERS:
STATES TAKING REFUGEES FROM ABROAD
1994 numbers

1 million

500,000

250,000

100,000

other states

Source: U.S. Committee for Refugees.

GREENLAND
(Den)

ICELAND

CANADA

NORWAY
SWEDEN

DENMARK

IRELAND
UNITED
KINGDOM

NETH
POLAN

BEL GERMANY CZECH

UNITED STATES
OF AMERICA

FRANCE
S
AUS
H

ITALY
B-H

PORTUGAL SPAIN

*ATLANTIC
OCEAN*

MOROCCO

TUNISIA

ALGERIA

LIB

MEXICO

CUBA
BAHAMAS

DOMINICAN
REPUBLIC

JAMAICA
BELIZE
HAITI

GUATEMALA
HONDURAS
EL SALVADOR
NICARAGUA

COSTA RICA
PANAMA

BARBADOS

TRINIDAD & TOBAGO

VENEZUELA
GUYANA
SURINAME
FRENCH GUIANA (Fr)

COLOMBIA

ECUADOR

WESTERN SAHARA

MAURITANIA
MALI
NIGER

SENEGAL
GAMBIA
GUINEA-BISSAU
GUINEA
SIERRA LEONE
LIBERIA

BURKINA
FASO
CÔTE d'
IVOIRE
GHANA
BENIN

CH

NIGERIA

TOGO
EQUATORIAL GUINEA
CAMEROON
C

GABON
CONGO

BRAZIL

PERU

BOLIVIA

PARAGUAY

CHILE

URUGUAY

ARGENTINA

ANGO

NAMIBIA

DEBT AT HOME:
BUDGET DEFICIT OR SURPLUS
AS PERCENTAGE OF GROSS
DOMESTIC PRODUCT
1993 or latest available date

deficit

-10%
-5%
-2.5%

surplus

+2.5%
+5%

no data

Biggest deficits: Greece, -29%; Ukraine, -28%;
Yemen, -19.8%; Georgia, -17.8%;
Guinea-Bissau, -17.7%
Biggest surpluses: Turkmenistan, +14%;
Botswana, +11.7%; Singapore, +9%

Sources: IMF; *Statistical Yearbook of the Republic
of China* (Taiwan); UN; press reports.

A DEGREE OF AID:
OFFICIAL DEVELOPMENT ASSISTANCE
1989-91 percentages of donor's
Gross National Product (GNP)

Source: World Resources Institute,
World Resources 1994-95.

Ireland, New Zealand,
Portugal, Spain, U.S.A.
0.2%

Austria, Japan, Switzerland, UK
0.3%

Australia, Germany, Italy, UAE
0.4%

Belgium, Canada, Kuwait
0.5%

France
0.6%

U.N.
recommendation

0.7%
of donor's GNP

Finland
0.7%

Netherlands
0.9%

Denmark, Sweden
1%

Norway
1.1%

Saudi
Arabia
2%

Governments frequently spend more than they collect in taxes. To finance deficits, they accumulate debt. To repay debt or meet interest payments, poor states sacrifice their export income.

RUSSIA

KAZAKHSTAN

MONGOLIA

UKRAINE

TURKEY

GEO

ARM AZER

UZBEKISTAN

KIRGISTAN

TURKMEN

TAJ

AFGHANISTAN

CHINA

N.KOREA

JAPAN

S.KOREA

SYRIA

LEB

ISRAEL JOR

IRAQ

IRAN

PAKISTAN

NEPAL

BHUTAN

B'DESH

TAIWAN

PACIFIC OCEAN

KUWAIT

BAHRAIN

QATAR UAE

SAUDI ARABIA

INDIA

OMAN

YEMEN

ERITREA

DJIBOUTI

MYANMAR

LAOS

VIETNAM

THAILAND

CAM

PHILIPPINES

EGYPT

SUDAN

ETHIOPIA

SOMALIA

UGANDA

KENYA

MALDIVES

SRI LANKA

BRUNEI

MALAYSIA

SINGAPORE

SEYCHELLES

TANZANIA

MALAWI

MADAGASCAR

MAURITIUS

MOZAMBIQUE

ZIMBABWE

INDONESIA

PAPUA NEW GUINEA

SOLOMON ISLANDS

VANUATU

AUSTRALIA

FIJI

TONGA

NEW ZEALAND

Uganda 87%
Algeria 71%
Guyana 62%

over 60%
3 countries

41-60%
8 countries

up to 10%
15 countries

20-40%
41 countries

10-20%
26 countries

DEBT ABROAD:
PERCENTAGE OF EXPORT INCOME
SPENT ON SERVICING FOREIGN DEBT
1989-91 93 states

Source: World Resources Institute,
World Resources 1994-95.

2.739%

GREENLAND
(Den)

ICELAND

NORWAY
SWEDEN

DENMARK

IRELAND
UNITED
KINGDOM

NETH
BEL GERMANY
CZECH
POLAND

FRANCE
S AUS HU
ITALY

PORTUGAL SPAIN

C A N A D A

UNITED STATES
OF AMERICA

MOROCCO
TUNISIA

ALGERIA
LIBY

WESTERN SAHARA

MAURITANIA
MALI
NIGER

MEXICO

BAHAMAS

CUBA
DOMINICAN
REPUBLIC

SENEGAL
GAMBIA
GUINEA
BISSAU GUINEA

BELIZE JAMAICA HAITI
HONDURAS
GUATEMALA
EL SALVADOR

ST KITTS NEVIS

BURKINA
FASO
BENIN
CÔTE d'
IVOIRE GHANA
NIGERIA
CH

SIERRA LEONE
LIBERIA

NICARAGUA

COSTA RICA
PANAMA

GRENADA BARBADOS
TRINIDAD & TOBAGO

VENEZUELA
GUYANA

TOGO
CAMEROON

EQUATORIAL GUINEA
SAO TOME & PRINCIPE
GABON
CONGO

PACIFIC
OCEAN

COLOMBIA

SURINAME
FRENCH GUIANA (Fr)

1.320%

ECUADOR

B R A Z I L

991%

PERU

ANGO

BOLIVIA

NAMIBIA

PARAGUAY

CHILE

414%

URUGUAY

ARGENTINA

295%

ANNUAL INFLATION
1992 or latest available date
percentages

rising prices

100%

50%

15%

5%

falling prices

no data

Sources: CIA; IMF; press reports.

156%

1981-1985
1986-1988
1989
1990
1991
1992

**BRAZIL'S
ANNUAL INFLATION**
1971-92 percentages
Sources: CIA; IMF.

Inflation victimizes the most vulnerable
in society who lack the means and
skills to exploit its distortions.
It is a classic way by which
the state effectively
repudiates
its debts.

In July 1993,
inflation in Yugoslavia (Serbia-
Montenegro) was 500% per month. By
January 1994, prices were rising faster than
100% per hour. The Yugoslav National Bank
produced a bright orange note of
500,000,000,000 Dinars.

RUSSIA

KAZAKHSTAN

MONGOLIA

N.KOREA   JAPAN

S.KOREA

TURKEY

SYRIA

IRAQ

IRAN

AFGHANISTAN

CHINA

PACIFIC
OCEAN

KUWAIT

BAHRAIN

QATAR   UAE

PAKISTAN

NEPAL   BHUTAN

TAIWAN

SAUDI ARABIA

OMAN

INDIA

B.
DESH

HONG KONG

MYANMAR   LAOS

VIETNAM

ERITREA

YEMEN

THAILAND

ETHIOPIA

SOMALIA

CAMBODIA

PHILIPPINES

UGANDA

KENYA

MALDIVES

SRI LANKA

BRUNEI

MALAYSIA

SINGAPORE

TANZANIA

SEYCHELLES

INDONESIA

PAPUA
NEW
GUINEA

COMOROS

MALAWI

MADAGASCAR

MAURITIUS

MOZAMBIQUE

AUSTRALIA

WESTERN SAMOA

FIJI
TONGA

1,445%

UKRAINE'S
ANNUAL INFLATION
1971-92 percentages
Sources: CIA; IMF.

NEW
ZEALAND

91.2%

1981-85 1.1%   1986-88 1.3%   1989 2.2%   1990 4.2%

1991

1992

British Sky Broadcasting
Austria
Belgium
Denmark
Finland
France
Israel
Netherlands
Norway
Sweden
Switzerland
UK
and elsewhere

Rupert Murdoch's News Corporation is one of a few media companies with a considerable international presence. Others include Time Warner (U.S.A.) and Bertelsmann (Germany).

Some major media companies are more renowned for their home dominance but have subsidiary interests elsewhere. These include Fininvest (Italy), whose proprietor, Silvio Berlusconi, was for a short period that country's prime minister; Globo (Brazil); and, Grupo Televisa (Mexico) the world's leading Spanish-language media conglomerate.

Sources: Belfield, Hird and Kelly; *The Economist;* News Corporation Limited; Shawcross; UN Environment Programme.

Star Television
Afghanistan
China
Hong Kong
India
Indonesia
Jordan
South Korea
Kuwait
Pakistan
Philippines
Saudi Arabia
Taiwan
Thailand
UEA

television
Australia
Luxembourg
U.S.A.

newspapers and magazines
Australia
Fiji
Germany
Hong Kong
New Zealand
Papua New Gunea
Spain
UK
U.S.A.

book publishing
Australia
UK
U.S.A.

film
U.S.A.

STATE ATTITUDES TO RELIGION
early 1990s

states with an official belief

others repressed

others tolerated

states with no official belief

favouritism in practice

even-handedness in practice

unknown or unclear

a religion receives substantial state funding

Sources: Barrett; O'Brien and Palmer;
personal communications.

FUNDAMENTALISM
1994

fundamentalist states

states challenged by fundamentalists

states where government policy is influenced by fundamentalists

states where government policy takes into account fundamentalist opinion

states where policy is not affected

unclear or unknown

Sources: Marty and Appleby; press reports;
personal communications.

Beliefs sustain the state. The state tries to sustain belief.

NEWSPAPER CIRCULATION
PER 100 PEOPLE
1987-92 or latest available date

20 newspapers per 100 people
10
5
2.5
1

no data

Highest: Hong Kong, 65; Norway, 61
Lowest: Burkina Faso, Chad, Rwanda, 0

OVER 10 TELEVISION SETS
PER 100 PEOPLE *1990*

over 40 television sets per 100 people

21-40

10-20

Most televisions: U.S.A., 81; Oman, 76; Malta, 74

Sources: U.N. Environmental Programme; World Bank,
Social Indicators of Development 1994.

Newspapers are in many states the major instrument for directly influencing political opinion, although television is perhaps the most potent form of mass communication.

RUSSIA

KAZAKHSTAN

MONGOLIA

N.KOREA

JAPAN

S.KOREA

CHINA

PACIFIC
OCEAN

GEO

AZER

RKEY

UZBEKISTAN

KIRGISTAN

SYRIA

DEB

TURKMEN

TAJ.

IRAQ

IRAN

AFGHANISTAN

AE / JOR

KUWAIT

BAHRAIN

PAKISTAN

TAIWAN

QATARY

UAE

NEPAL

BHUTAN

SAUDI
ARABIA

OMAN

INDIA

B
DESH

MYANMAR

LAOS

HONG
KONG

YEMEN

VIETNAM

ERITREA

THAI

CAM

PHILIPPINES

DJIBOUTI

ETHIOPIA

SOMALIA

MALDIVES

SRI LANKA

BRUNEI

UGANDA

KENYA

MALAYSIA

SEYCHELLES

SINGAPORE

TANZANIA

INDONESIA

PAPUA
NEW
GUINEA

MALAWI

MADAGASCAR

MAURITIUS

MOZAMBIQUE

AUSTRALIA

FIJI

TONGA

CANADA

RUSSIA

NEW
ZEALAND

UNITED STATES
OF AMERICA

KAZAKHSTAN

MONGOLIA

TURKEY

CHINA

JAPAN

IRAN

ALGERIA

LIBYA

INDIA

SUDAN

RADIOS PER 100 PEOPLE *1990*

ZAIRE

BRAZIL

INDONESIA

100 per 100 people

75

50

25

AUSTRALIA

no data

Source: U.N. Environmental Programme.

Most radios: U.S.A., 212; Australia, 128; UK, 114
Least radios: Bhutan, 2

CANADA

GREENLAND
(Den)

UNITED STATES
OF AMERICA

ICELAND

NORWAY

SWEDEN

DENMARK

UNITED
KINGDOM

IRELAND

NETH.

POLA

BEL

GERMANY

CZECH

FRANCE

AUS

ITALY

PORTUGAL   SPAIN

MALTA

MEXICO

BAHAMAS

CUBA

DOMINICAN
REPUBLIC

JAMAICA

HAITI

ANTIGUA AND
BARBUDA

BELIZE

HONDURAS

ST. KITTS NEVIS
ANGUILLA

GUATEMALA

DOMINICA

EL SALVADOR

ST. VINCENT &
GRENADINES

ST. LUCIA

NICARAGUA

GRENADA

COSTA RICA

TRINIDAD & TOBAGO

PANAMA

VENEZUELA

GUYANA

SURINAME

FRENCH GUIANA (Fr)

COLOMBIA

ECUADOR

ATLANTIC
OCEAN

MOROCCO

ALGERIA

LIB

WESTERN SAHARA

MAURITANIA

MALI

NIGER

SENEGAL

GAMBIA

BURKINA
FASO

GUINEA-BISSAU

GUINEA

CÔTE d'
IVOIRE

GHANA

BENIN

NIGERIA

SIERRA LEONE

TOGO

CAMEROON

LIBERIA

EQUATORIAL GUINEA

SAO TOME & PRINCIPE

GABON

CONGO

BRAZIL

PERU

BOLIVIA

PARAGUAY

CHILE

URUGUAY

ARGENTINA

ANGO

NAMIB

CENSORSHIP:
STATES' INFRINGEMENTS OF
FREEDOMS OF BELIEF, EXPRESSION,
COMMUNICATION AND MOVEMENT
early 1990s

draconian
*imprisonment, or worse, for holding
views hostile to the state or its
representatives, or withholding public
support for them*

severe
*punishment is common for expressing
hostility to the state or its representatives*

mild
*laws governing the expression of opinion
are usually in abeyance, except in times
of war*

unclear or unknown

situation worsening *end 1994*

situation improving *end 1994*

Sources: *Index on Censorship;* U.S. State Department.

All states abridge their citizens' freedoms: to hold opinions, to express them, and to travel. Some set the limits wide, some narrow.

RUSSIA

KAZAKHSTAN

MONGOLIA

KIRGISTAN

UZBEKISTAN

TURKMEN

TAJ.

N.KOREA

JAPAN

S KOREA

CHINA

GEO.
AZER.
ARM
'URKEY

SYRIA
DEB
IRAQ

IRAN

AFGHANISTAN

KUWAIT
BAHRAIN
QATAR UAE

PAKISTAN

NEPAL

BHUTAN

B
'DESH

TAIWAN

HONG KONG

PACIFIC
OCEAN

SAUDI ARABIA

OMAN

INDIA

MYANMAR

LAOS

VIETNAM

THAILAND

CAM

ERITREA
YEMEN
DJIBOUTI

ETHIOPIA

SOMALIA

MALDIVES

SRI LANKA

PHILIPPINES

KIRIBATI

MARSHALL
ISLANDS

UGANDA
KENYA

BRUNEI

MALAYSIA

SINGAPORE

NAURU

RUNDI
TANZANIA

SEYCHELLES

INDONESIA

PAPUA
NEW
GUINEA

SOLOMON
ISLANDS

COMOROS

MALAWI

MADAGASCAR

MAURITIUS

MOZAMBIQUE

PRISONERS OF CONSCIENCE
January 1994

Amnesty International prisoners of
conscience and/or International PEN cases

other states

AUSTRALIA

WESTERN SAMOA

FIJI
TONGA

GREENLAND
(Den)

CANADA

RUSSIA

KAZAKHSTAN MONGOLIA

UNITED STATES
OF AMERICA

TURKEY

JAPAN

IRAN

CHINA

ALGERIA LIBYA

INDIA

SUDAN

NEW
ZEALAND

ZAIRE

BRAZIL

INDONESIA

AUSTRALIA

115

Sources: Amnesty International; International PEN.

ICELAND

NORWAY SWEDEN FINLAND

ESTONIA
LATVIA
LITH
BELARUS

DEN

IRELAND

UNITED
KINGDOM

NETH
BEL GERMANY POLAND
CZ SLO UKRAINE
AUS HUNG MOL
FRANCE SW S C ROMANIA
ITALY B-H YUG
BULG
ALB M

PORTUGAL SPAIN GREECE TURK

C A N A D A

UNITED STATES
OF AMERICA

BERMUDA

A T L A N T I C
O C E A N

MEXICO

BAHAMAS

CUBA
DOMINICAN
REPUBLIC
JAMAICA HAITI
BELIZE
HONDURAS
GUATEMALA
EL SALVADOR
NICARAGUA
COSTA RICA
PANAMA

DOMINICA
ST. LUCIA
GRENADA BARBADOS
TRINIDAD & TOBAGO

VENEZUELA
GUYANA
SURINAME
FRENCH GUIANA (Fr)

COLOMBIA

ECUADOR

P A C I F I C
O C E A N

PERU

B R A Z I L

BOLIVIA

CHILE PARAGUAY

URUGUAY

ARGENTINA

MOROCCO

WESTERN SAHARA

ALGERIA

LIB

TUNISIA

MAURITANIA

MALI

NIGER

C

CAPE VERDE

SENEGAL
GAMBIA
GUINEA-BISSAU
GUINEA

SIERRA LEONE
LIBERIA

BURKINA
FASO
CÔTE d'
IVOIRE
GHANA
BENIN
TOGO

NIGERIA

CAMEROON

EQUATORIAL GUINEA
GABON
CONGO

ANGO

NAMIBI

RELATIVE POWER OF THE MAIN
INTERNATIONAL LANGUAGES
early 1990s millions of speakers

home language is official language

home language differs from official
language

Source: Gunnemark.

30m 160m Portuguese 190m
35m 200m Arabic 235m
185m 65m French 250m
30m 300m Spanish 330m

1,400m

SHARES OF POPULATION FOR WHOM
THEIR HOME LANGUAGE
IS NOT AN OFFICIAL LANGUAGE
early 1990s percentages

90%
75%
50%
25%
10%

no data

Source: Gunnemark.

Only 80 of the world's 5,300 or so languages are official languages.

RUSSIA

KAZAKHSTAN

MONGOLIA

N.KOREA   JAPAN

UZBEKISTAN   CHINA

KIRGISTAN

S.KOREA

AZER   TURKMEN   TAJ

IRAQ   IRAN   AFGHANISTAN

KUWAIT

BAHRAIN

QATAR   UAE

SAUDI ARABIA   OMAN

YEMEN

ERITREA

DJIBOUTI

ETHIOPIA

SOMALIA

NEPAL

BHUTAN

B DESH

INDIA

MYANMAR

LAOS

THAILAND

CAM

VIETNAM

TAIWAN

HONG KONG

PACIFIC
OCEAN

PHILIPPINES

KIRIBATI

MARSHALL
ISLANDS

MICRONESIA

MALDIVES

SRI LANKA

BRUNEI

MALAYSIA

SINGAPORE

NAURU

INDONESIA

PAPUA
NEW
GUINEA

SOLOMON
ISLANDS

UGANDA

KENYA

TANZANIA

COMOROS

SEYCHELLES

MADAGASCAR

MAURITIUS

MALAWI

MOZAMBIQUE

VANUATU

NEW CALEDONIA

AUSTRALIA

FIJI

COOK ISLANDS

TONGA

NEW
ZEALAND

**GOLDEN TONGUES:
LANGUAGES OF INTERNATIONAL
TRADE AND TOURISM** *early 1990s*

- English
- French
- mixed or other
- no data

CANADA

UNITED STATES
OF AMERICA

RUSSIA

KAZAKHSTAN   MONGOLIA

TURKEY   JAPAN

ALGERIA   LIBYA

IRAN   CHINA

SUDAN   INDIA

ZAIRE

BRAZIL

INDONESIA

AUSTRALIA

English
1,730m

Source: Gunnemark.

117

ICELAND

NORWAY   SWEDEN   FINLAND

ESTONIA

DENMARK   LATVIA
LITH

IRELAND   UNITED   POLAND   BELA
KINGDOM   NETH

BEL   GERMANY   UKRA
CZECH
REPUBLIC
SLOVAK

AUSTRIA   HUNGARY
FRANCE   SWITZ   SLO   ROMA
CROATIA
B - H   YUG
ITALY   BULGA
PORTUGAL   ALB   M
SPAIN   GREECE

6 provinces

C A N A D A

20 states   7 states

UNITED STATES
OF AMERICA

MOROCCO   TUNISIA

BERMUDA   A T L A N T I C
O C E A N   ALGERIA   LIB

MEXICO   WESTERN SAHARA
BAHAMAS

CUBA   DOMINICAN
REPUBLIC   MAURITANIA   MALI   NIGER
CAPE VERDE
ANTIGUA & BARBUDA
BELIZE   JAMAICA   HAITI   SENEGAL
GUATEMALA   HONDURAS   ST LUCIA   GAMBIA   BURKINA   CH
EL SALVADOR   BARBADOS   GUINEA-BISSAU   FASO
NICARAGUA   TRINIDAD & TOBAGO   GUINEA   NIGERIA
COSTA RICA   VENEZUELA   SIERRA LEONE   CÔTE d'   GHANA BENIN
PANAMA   GUYANA   LIBERIA   IVOIRE
SURINAME   TOGO   CAMEROON
FRENCH GUIANA (Fr)   EQUATORIAL GUINEA
COLOMBIA   GABON
P A C I F I C   CONGO
O C E A N   ECUADOR

SEX AND THE SINGLE NORM:
TREATMENT OF HOMOSEXUALITY   ANGO
1994   B R A Z I L
PERU

legal   NAMIBIA
BOLIVIA
legal with some discriminatory
provisions   PARAGUAY
CHILE
legal but repressed

illegal but tolerated   URUGUAY
ARGENTINA
illegal and repressed

legal position unknown but reported
social hostility

federal systems with varying attitudes

no data   Brazil
30
only male homosexuality targeted   U.S.A.
in law or in practice   **22**   Colombia   Australia
oral and anal sex illegal, regardless of gender   **18**   **16**   Peru   In
13   **10**
discrimination against homosexuality illegal

STATES WHERE 10 OR
MORE LANGUAGES HAVE
BECOME EXTINCT
by mid-1980s
Source: *The Third Pink Book.*   number of languages

Source: Grimes.

118

States want their citizens to conform. Sexual expression and language are just two areas in which societies seek to suppress differences.

EXTINCT LANGUAGES:
LANGUAGES NO LONGER SPOKEN
AS MOTHER TONGUE *mid-1980s*

- some languages now extinct
- some languages nearly extinct, or only a few elderly speakers
- one or more languages may be extinct
- not applicable or no data

2 states   4 states/territories

Source: Grimes.

Even key social indices, such as mortality rates of
children under five years old, numbers of malnourished
children, and children in primary education, are for many
states likely to be inadequate or dated. The bar chart
shows – for 100 states in Africa, Asia, Central and South
America, and the Caribbean – the age of data
internationally available for these indices in 1993.

Poor states are more likely than rich ones to lack the
necessary resources to collect and organize information
regularly. Government policy may not rate the provision
of data as important enough for the investment of scarce
resources. Indeed, governments may sometimes refuse to
make such data public, regarding it as likely to prove
more embarrassing than useful.

Statistics may be up to date but still unreliable. By their
very selectiveness, in rich states as well as poor ones,
statistics may mislead rather than reveal.

Source: UNICEF, *The Progress of Nations*, 1994.

45 states

28 states

18 states

4 states

3-4 years old   5-9 years old   10-14 years old   15 years old

GREENLAND
(Den)

ICELAND

NORWAY
SWEDEN

DENMARK

IRELAND
UNITED
KINGDOM

POLAN

NETH
BEL
GERMANY
CZEC

FRANCE
AUS
HU

ITALY

PORTUGAL
SPAIN
VATICAN
AL

GR

GIBRALTAR
MALTA

C A N A D A

MOROCCO

TUNISIA

LIBY

ALGERIA

UNITED STATES
OF AMERICA

WESTERN SAHARA

MAURITANIA
MALI
NIGER
CH

MEXICO

BERMUDA

BAHAMAS

BELIZE
GUATEMALA
HONDURAS
EL SALVADOR
NICARAGUA
COSTA RICA
PANAMA

CUBA

JAMAICA

DOMINICAN
REPUBLIC

HAITI
PUERTO
RICO (U.S.)

CAPE
VERDE

SENEGAL
GAMBIA
GUINEA-BISSAU

BURKINA
FASO

BENIN

NIGERIA

ST. KITTS
NEVIS

ANTIGUA
& BARBUDA

GUADELOUPE (Fr)

DOMINICA

MARTINIQUE (Fr)

ST. LUCIA

ST. VINCENT &
GRENADINES

BARBADOS

GRENADA

GUINEA

SIERRA LEONE

CÔTE d'
IVOIRE

GHANA

TOGO

CA

LIBERIA

VENEZUELA

GUYANA

SURINAME

FRENCH
GUYANA (Fr)

TRINIDAD
& TOBAGO

EQUATORIAL GUINEA

SAO TOME & PRINCIPE

CAMEROON

GABON

CONGO

Z

COLOMBIA

ECUADOR

PACIFIC
OCEAN

PERU

BRAZIL

ANGOL

BOLIVIA

PARAGUAY

CHILE

NAMIBIA

URUGUAY

S
A

ARGENTINA

FALKLAND
ISLANDS (UK)

**CURRENTLY RECOGNIZED
SOVEREIGN STATES** *1995*
uninterrupted independence since:

1990-1993

1960-1989

1940-1959

1915-1939

1800-1914

pre-1800

occupied and dependent territories or
other anomalies

privileged zone: extended economic zone
or exclusive fishing zone *schematic*

Sources: *Statesman's Year-Book 1993-94;*
U.S. State Department; press reports.

States exist only in each other's recognition, yet they divide the earth and its waters between them. Big or small they pretend to permanence, yet are a blink in history.

RUSSIA

KAZAKHSTAN

MONGOLIA

N KOREA   JAPAN

S KOREA

PACIFIC OCEAN

TURKEY

SYRIA
DEB

IRAQ

IRAN

AFGHANISTAN

CHINA

KUWAIT

BAHRAIN

PAKISTAN

QATAR   UAE

NEPAL   BHUTAN

SAUDI ARABIA

OMAN

INDIA

B.
DESH

MYANMAR   LAOS

TAIWAN

HONG KONG

YEMEN

ERITREA

DJIBOUTI

VIETNAM

THAILAND

ETHIOPIA

SOMALIA

CAM

PHILIPPINES

MALDIVES

SRI LANKA

BRUNEI

UGANDA

KENYA

MALAYSIA

SINGAPORE

MICRONESIA

TANZANIA   SEYCHELLES

COMOROS

INDONESIA

PAPUA
NEW
GUINEA

MALAWI

MADAGASCAR

MOZAMBIQUE   MAURITIUS

AUSTRALIA

NEW ZEALAND

■ MARSHALL ISLANDS
■ KIRIBATI
■ NAURU

SOLOMON
ISLANDS ■

VANUATU

FIJI ■   ■ WESTERN SAMOA

□ TONGA   □ COOK
ISLANDS

NEW CALEDONIA

	1 International frontiers 1994 kms		2 Population mid-1993 millions	3 Young and old people 1994 percentage of population		4 Population density 1993 people per
	land	coastline		under 15 years	over 65 years	
Afghanistan	5,529	0	17.4	46%	4%	32.2
Albania	720	362	3.3	33%	5%	114.8
Algeria	6,343	998	27.3	44%	4%	10.8
Angola	5,198	1,600	9.5	45%	3%	7.6
Argentina	9,665	4,989	33.5	30%	9%	11.8
Armenia	1,254	0	3.6	30%	5%	120.3
Australia	0	25,760	17.8	22%	11%	2.2
Austria	2,496	0	7.9	18%	15%	93.3
Azerbaijan	2,013	0	7.2	33%	5%	83.6
Bahamas	0	3,542	0.3	30%	5%	18.7
Bahrain	0	161	0.5	35%	2%	758.8
Bangladesh	4,246	580	113.9	44%	3%	778.8
Barbados	0	97	0.3	25%	11%	600.2
Belarus	3,098	0	10.3	23%	10%	49.5
Belgium	1,385	64	10.1	18%	15%	-
Belize	516	386	0.2	44%	5%	8.5
Benin	1,989	121	5.1	46%	3%	43.4
Bhutan	1,878	0	0.8	39%	4%	31.2
Bolivia	6,743	0	8.0	41%	4%	6.7
Bosnia-Herzegovina	1,459	20	4.0	28%	6%	-
Botswana	4,013	0	1.4	48%	3%	2.3
Brazil	14,691	7,491	152.0	35%	5%	17.8
Brunei	381	161	0.3	36%	3%	45.9
Bulgaria	1,808	354	9.0	20%	13%	77.3
Burkina Faso	3,192	0	10.0	48%	4%	33.8
Burundi	974	0	5.8	46%	4%	203.1
Cambodia	2,572	443	9.0	35%	3%	48.8
Cameroon	4,591	402	12.8	45%	3%	25
Canada	8,893	243,791	28.1	21%	12%	2.7
Central African Rep.	5,203	0	3.1	42%	3%	5
Chad	5,968	0	5.4	41%	4%	4.5
Chile	6,171	6,435	13.5	31%	6%	17.7
China	22,143	14,500	1,178.5	28%	6%	120.
Colombia	7,408	3,208	34.9	34%	4%	28.8
Comoros	0	340	0.5	48%	3%	220.
Congo	5,504	169	2.4	44%	3%	6.9
Costa Rica	639	1,290	3.3	37%	5%	60.9
Côte d'Ivoire	3,110	515	13.4	48%	3%	38.
Croatia	2,028	5,790	4.4	21%	12%	84.
Cuba	29	3,735	11.0	23%	9%	96.
Cyprus	0	648	0.7	26%	10%	76.
Czech Republic	1,880	0	10.3	21%	13%	
Denmark	68	3,379	5.2	17%	16%	119.

Sources: Col 1: *CIA, World Factbook 1994;* **Cols 2 and 3:** Population Concern, *1993 World Population Data Sheet;* **Cols 4 and 5:** World Bank, *Social Indicators of Development 1994;* **Col 6:** *World Bank Atlas 1995;* **Col 7:** Krishna Ahooja-Patel, 1993. The index is based on seven indicators: income,

WORLD TABLE

5 Number of people per hospital bed 1994	6 Purchasing power per person 1993 U.S. dollars	7 Women's advancement 1993 index (1= best)	8 Number of cars 1993 thousands	9 Number of letters and cards posted per person 1992	
4,003	–	107	55.0	–	Afghanistan
246	340	–	48.9	–	Albania
400	1,650	70	1,535.0	12.72	Algeria
771	–	–	147.5	0.08	Angola
216	7,290	28	5,835.0	0.59	Argentina
120	660	–	14.8	–	Armenia
183	17,510	–	9,954.5	195.23	Australia
94	23,120	–	3,563.0	–	Austria
101	730	–	355.2	–	Azerbaijan
227	11,500	–	–	–	Bahamas
302	7,870	–	140.3	–	Bahrain
3,158	220	97	99.0	1.43	Bangladesh
117	6,240	–	–	34.79	Barbados
8	2,840	–	–	–	Belarus
121	21,210	13	4,482.6	123.31	Belgium
185	2,440	–	–	–	Belize
886	420	77	34.0	0.76	Benin
–	170	102	–	0.95	Bhutan
828	770	87	230.0	0.86	Bolivia
–	–	–	–	–	Bosnia-Herzegovina
421	2,590	42	71.6	–	Botswana
301	3,020	36	12,950.0	18.12	Brazil
319	–	–	128.4	26.11	Brunei
100	1,160	–	1,489.0	24.03	Bulgaria
3,392	300	88	23.5	1.20	Burkina Faso
890	180	68	18.0	0.44	Burundi
478	–	108	30.0	–	Cambodia
393	770	48	165.0	–	Cameroon
64	20,670	3	17,014.5	–	Canada
1,171	390	91	20.0	–	Central African Rep.
1,373	200	105	15.0	0.30	Chad
320	3,070	24	1,167.7	17.81	Chile
388	490	23	6,988.8	4.88	China
703	1,400	38	1,470.0	–	Colombia
476	520	–	–	–	Comoros
228	920	64	46.0	–	Congo
302	2,160	26	178.9	3.97	Costa Rica
1,269	630	66	255.0	2.78	Côte d'Ivoire
–	–	–	–	–	Croatia
207	–	–	47.0	–	Cuba
180	10,380	–	298.8	–	Cyprus
–	2,730	–	3,460.7	110.04	Czech Republic
177	26,510	2	1,917.0	214.87	Denmark

ternal mortality, infant mortality, life expectancy, post-secondary school enrolment, share of paid employment and participation in national parliament; **◀ 8:** Motor Industry of Great Britain, *World Resources 1994-95;* **Col 9:** Union Postale Universelle, *Statistique des services postaux 1992.*

	1 International Frontiers 1994 kms		2 Population mid-1993 millions	3 Young and old people 1994 percentage of population		4 Populati density 1993 people per
	land	coastline		under 15 years	over 65 years	
Djibouti	508	314	0.5	45%	3%	22.5
Dominican Republic	275	1,288	7.6	38%	3%	147.7
Ecuador	2,010	2,237	10.3	39%	4%	38
Egypt	2,689	3,450	58.3	39%	4%	53.5
El Salvador	545	307	5.2	45%	4%	250.9
Equatorial Guinea	539	296	0.4	43%	4%	15.2
Eritrea	1,630	1,151	–	–	–	–
Estonia	557	1,393	1.6	22%	12%	34.7
Ethiopia	5,311	0	56.7	49%	4%	43.3
Fiji	0	1,129	0.8	38%	3%	40.
Finland	2,628	1,126	5.1	19%	14%	14.8
France	2,892	3,427	57.7	20%	14%	103.5
Gabon	2,551	885	1.1	33%	6%	4.4
Gambia	740	80	0.9	44%	3%	84.8
Georgia	1,461	310	5.5	25%	9%	78.6
Germany	3,621	2,389	81.1	16%	15%	224.1
Ghana	2,093	539	16.4	45%	3%	64.2
Greece	1,210	13,676	10.5	19%	14%	77.
Guatemala	1,687	400	10.0	45%	3%	86.9
Guinea	3,399	320	6.2	44%	3%	24.
Guinea Bissau	724	350	1.0	43%	3%	27.7
Guyana	2,462	459	0.8	35%	4%	3.7
Haiti	275	1,771	6.5	40%	4%	237.0
Honduras	1,520	820	5.6	47%	4%	46.9
Hong Kong	30	733	5.8	21%	9%	5,533.7
Hungary	1,989	0	10.3	20%	13%	111.2
Iceland	0	4,988	0.3	25%	11%	2.5
India	14,103	7,000	897.4	36%	4%	263.0
Indonesia	2,602	54,716	187.6	37%	4%	95.2
Iran	5,440	2,440	62.8	47%	3%	3
Iraq	3,631	58	19.2	48%	3%	42.
Ireland	360	1,448	3.6	27%	11%	50.
Israel	1,006	273	5.3	31%	9%	238.
Italy	1,899	4,996	57.8	17%	14%	191.
Jamaica	0	1,022	2.4	33%	8%	216.
Japan	0	29,791	124.8	18%	13%	32
Jordan	1,619	26	3.8	44%	3%	41.
Kazakhstan	12,012	0	17.2	32%	6%	6.
Kenya	3,446	536	27.7	49%	2%	4
Kirgistan	3,878	0	4.6	37%	5%	22.
Korea (North)	1,673	2,495	22.6	29%	4%	184.
Korea (South)	238	2,413	44.6	26%	5%	43
Kuwait	464	499	1.7	42%	1%	81.

Sources: Col 1: *CIA, World Factbook 1994;* **Cols 2 and 3:** Population Concern, *1993 World Population Data Sheet;* **Cols 4 and 5:** World Bank, *Social Indicators of Development 1994;* **Col 6:** *World Bank Atlas1995;* **Col 7:** Krishna Ahooja-Patel, 1993. The index is based on seven indicators: income,

5 Number of people per hospital bed 1994	6 Purchasing power per person 1993 U.S. dollars	7 Women's advancement 1993 index (1 = best)	8 Number of cars 1993 thousands	9 Number of letters and cards posted per person 1992	
265	780	–	15.0	–	Djibouti
529	1,080	58	245.0	–	Dominican Republic
625	1,170	57	240.0	0.78	Ecuador
536	660	78	1,585.0	2.88	Egypt
699	1,320	55	255.1	1.11	El Salvador
–	360	–	–	–	Equatorial Guinea
–	–	–	–	–	Eritrea
82	3,040	–	366.4	–	Estonia
4,141	100	98	52.5	–	Ethiopia
364	2,140	–	65.0	26.05	Fiji
93	18,970	6	2,230.6	81.89	Finland
109	22,360	5	29,060.0	210.25	France
800	4,050	47	40.0	–	Gabon
613	360	–	8.0	–	Gambia
90	560	–	–	–	Georgia
118	23,560	18	42,009.6	99.41	Germany
685	430	84	124.0	5.13	Ghana
196	7,390	–	2,533.3	31.74	Greece
673	1,110	51	295.0	5.99	Guatemala
1,816	510	99	27.5	–	Guinea
538	220	–	5.0	–	Guinea Bissau
300	350	–	31.0	–	Guyana
1,323	–	65	50.0	26.86	Haiti
993	580	49	77.5	–	Honduras
234	17,860	12	451.3	111.86	Hong Kong
99	3,330	–	2,234.5	82.31	Hungary
–	23,620	–	136.1	122.76	Iceland
1,371	290	76	4,667.7	12.82	India
1,503	730	72	3,088.7	1.73	Indonesia
724	2,230	81	2,100.6	–	Iran
603	–	44	775.0	1.61	Iraq
101	12,580	15	1,013.6	123.89	Ireland
219	13,760	16	1,060.0	73.91	Israel
133	19,620	10	32,347.42	59.05	Italy
293	1,390	31	112.5	20.50	Jamaica
64	31,450	14	61,658.1	190.10	Japan
519	1,190	52	248.3	9.41	Jordan
75	1,540	–	–	–	Kazakhstan
623	270	61	310.0	14.05	Kenya
85	830	–	–	–	Kirgistan
–	–	–	–	–	Korea (North)
300	7,670	34	5,231.0	50.36	Korea (South)
241	23,350	20	560.0	–	Kuwait

ternal mortality, infant mortality, life expectancy, post-secondary school enrolment, share of paid employment and participation in national parliament; **l 8:** Motor Industry of Great Britain, *World Resources 1994-95;* **Col 9:** Union Postale Universelle, *Statistique des services postaux 1992.*

	1 International frontiers 1994 kms		2 Population mid-1993 millions	3 Young and old people 1994 percentage of population		4 Populati density 1993 people per
	land	coastline		under 15 years	over 65 years	
Laos	5,803	0	4.6	45%	4%	18
Latvia	1,078	531	2.6	21%	12%	41.3
Lebanon	454	225	3.6	40%	5%	356.5
Lesotho	909	0	1.9	41%	4%	59.7
Liberia	1,585	579	2.8	46%	4%	24.2
Libya	4,383	1,770	4.2	50%	2%	2.7
Lithuania	1,273	108	3.8	23%	11%	57.6
Luxembourg	359	0	0.4	17%	13%	
Macedonia	748	0	2.0	29%	7%	
Madagascar	0	4,828	13.3	47%	3%	20.5
Malawi	2,881	0	10.0	48%	3%	74.2
Malaysia	2,669	4,675	18.4	37%	4%	55.1
Mali	7,243	0	8.9	46%	4%	
Malta	0	140	0.4	23%	11%	1,115.0
Marshall Islands	0	370	0.1	51%	3%	
Mauritania	5,074	754	2.2	44%	4%	2
Mauritius	0	177	1.1	30%	5%	532.8
Mexico	4,538	9,330	90.0	38%	4%	42.5
Moldova	1,389	0	4.4	28%	8%	129.3
Mongolia	8,114	0	2.3	44%	4%	1.4
Morocco	2,002	1,835	28.0	40%	4%	57.4
Mozambique	4,571	2,470	15.3	44%	3%	20.
Myanmar	5,876	1,930	43.5	37%	4%	63.3
Namibia	3,824	1,572	1.6	46%	3%	1.8
Nepal	2,926	0	20.4	42%	3%	137.8
Netherlands	1,027	451	15.2	18%	13%	403.3
New Zealand	0	15,134	3.4	23%	12%	12.4
Nicaragua	1,231	910	4.1	46%	3%	2
Niger	5,697	0	8.5	49%	3%	6.3
Nigeria	4,047	853	95.1	45%	3%	107.
Norway	2,515	21,925	4.3	20%	16%	13.
Oman	1,374	2,092	1.6	47%	3%	7.
Pakistan	6,774	1,046	122.4	44%	4%	145.
Panama	555	2,490	2.5	35%	5%	3
Papua New Guinea	820	5,152	3.9	40%	3%	8.
Paraguay	3,920	0	4.2	40%	4%	10.
Peru	6,940	2,414	22.9	38%	4%	17.
Philippines	0	36,289	64.6	39%	4%	209.
Poland	3,114	491	38.5	25%	10%	122.
Portugal	1,214	1,793	9.8	21%	13%	106.
Qatar	60	563	0.5	28%	1%	45.
Romania	2,508	225	23.2	23%	11%	96.
Russia	20,139	37,653	149.0	23%	11%	8.

Sources: Col 1: *CIA, World Factbook 1994;* **Cols 2 and 3:** Population Concern, *1993 World Population Data Sheet;* **Cols 4 and 5:** World Bank, *Social Indicators of Development 1994;* **Col 6:** *World Bank 1995;* **Col 7:** Krishna Ahooja-Patel, 1993. The index is based on seven indicators: income,

5 nber of people per ospital bed 1994	6 Purchasing power per person 1993 U.S. dollars	7 Women's advancement 1993 index (1 = best)	8 Number of cars 1993 thousands	9 Number of letters and cards posted per person 1992	
399	290	62	17.0	0.18	Laos
72	2,030	–	411.7	23.60	Latvia
230	–	59	179.3	–	Lebanon
597	660	39	–	–	Lesotho
607	–	74	10.0	–	Liberia
246	–	80	800.0	–	Libya
79	1,310	–	657.4	11.00	Lithuania
84	35,850	–	214.4	315.55	Luxembourg
–	780	–	–	–	Macedonia
1,140	240	75	85.0	1.99	Madagascar
645	220	94	25.0	–	Malawi
430	3,160	27	430.7	38.73	Malaysia
1,400	300	103	26.0	–	Mali
100	–	–	–	78.51	Malta
–	–	–	–	–	Marshall Islands
1,278	510	101	11.5	–	Mauritania
300	2,980	37	73.6	19.55	Mauritius
801	3,750	32	10,398.7	6.29	Mexico
77	1,180	–	242.3	–	Moldova
87	400	–	46.9	–	Mongolia
309	1,030	79	775.0	6.84	Morocco
1,280	80	63	45.0	–	Mozambique
1,591	–	–	65.0	1.51	Myanmar
–	1,660	–	109.9	41.20	Namibia
4,010	160	93	–	1.49	Nepal
170	20,710	11	6,303.2	–	Netherlands
149	12,900	–	1,902.8	–	New Zealand
538	360	33	64.0	–	Nicaragua
1,974	270	95	35.0	0.46	Niger
599	310	89	1,350.0	3.09	Nigeria
211	26,340	1	1,961.1	128.16	Norway
558	5,600	67	195.0	–	Oman
1,769	430	90	1,027.4	5.61	Pakistan
300	2,580	25	223.6	1.61	Panama
299	1,120	73	39.0	–	Papua New Guinea
1,087	1,500	60	94.0	0.68	Paraguay
708	1,490	53	671.5	0.55	Peru
780	830	35	1,290.0	13.89	Philippines
153	2,270	–	7,889.9	25.04	Poland
816	7,890	–	2,715.7	65.64	Portugal
340	15,140	–	170.0	–	Qatar
113	1,120	–	1,971.7	11.32	Romania
73	2,350	–	27,500.0	19.67	Russia

ternal mortality, infant mortality, life expectancy, post-secondary school enrolment, share of paid employment and participation in national parliament;
◀ **8:** Motor Industry of Great Britain, *World Resources 1994-95*; **Col 9:** Union Postale Universelle, *Statistique des services postaux 1992*.

	1 International frontiers 1994 kms		2 Population mid-1993 millions	3 Young and old people 1994 percentage of population		4 Population density 1993 people per
	land	coastline		under 15 years	over 65 years	
Rwanda	893	0	7.4	49%	2%	271.1
Saudi Arabia	4,415	2,640	17.5	39%	2%	7.6
Senegal	2,640	531	7.9	47%	3%	38.8
Seychelles	0	491	0.1	35%	6%	245
Sierra Leone	958	402	4.5	44%	3%	59.1
Singapore	0	193	2.8	23%	6%	4,456.5
Slovak Republic	1,355	0	5.3	25%	10%	49.04
Slovenia	1,045	32	2.0	21%	11%	98.9
Solomon Islands	0	5,313	0.3	47%	3%	11.3
Somalia	2,366	3025	9.5	46%	3%	12.6
South Africa	4,750	2,798	39.0	40%	4%	31.8
Spain	1,903	4,964	39.1	19%	14%	77.3
Sri Lanka	0	1,340	17.8	35%	4%	262.9
Sudan	7,687	853	27.4	46%	2%	10.3
Suriname	1,707	386	0.4	41%	4%	2.5
Swaziland	535	0	0.8	47%	3%	47.6
Sweden	2,205	3,218	8.7	19%	18%	19.2
Switzerland	1,852	0	7.0	17%	15%	165.2
Syria	2,253	193	13.5	49%	4%	67.7
Tajikistan	3,657	0	5.7	43%	4%	38
Taiwan	0	1,448	20.9	26%	7%	
Tanzania	3,402	1,424	27.8	47%	3%	26.2
Thailand	4,863	3,219	57.2	29%	5%	111.4
Togo	1,647	56	4.1	49%	2%	66.4
Trinidad & Tobago	0	362	1.3	31%	6%	244.3
Tunisia	1,424	1,148	8.6	37%	5%	50.4
Turkey	2,627	7,200	60.7	35%	4%	73.6
Turkmenistan	3,736	1,768	4.0	41%	4%	7.3
Uganda	2,698	0	18.1	49%	3%	71.4
Ukraine	4,558	2,782	51.9	22%	12%	86.
United Arab Emirates	867	1,318	2.1	35%	1%	19.
United Kingdom	360	12,429	58.0	19%	16%	235.
United States	12,248	19,924	258.3	22%	13%	2
Uruguay	1,564	660	3.2	26%	12%	17.
Uzbekistan	6,221	0	21.7	41%	4%	46.
Venezuela	4,993	2,800	20.7	37%	4%	21.
Vietnam	3,818	3,444	71.8	39%	5%	204.
Western Sahara	–	–	0.2	–	–	
Yemen	1,746	1,906	11.3	49%	3%	2.
Yugoslavia	2,246	199	9.8	23%	11%	418.
Zaire	10,271	37	41.2	43%	3%	16.
Zambia	5,664	0	8.6	49%	2%	10.
Zimbabwe	3,066	0	10.7	45%	3%	25

Sources: Col 1: *CIA, World Factbook 1994;* **Cols 2 and 3:** Population Concern, *1993 World Population Data Sheet;* **Cols 4 and 5:** World Bank, *Social Indicators of Development 1994;* **Col 6:** *World Bank Atlas 1995;* **Col 7:** Krishna Ahooja-Patel, 1993. The index is based on seven indicators: income,

5 Number of people per hospital bed 1994	6 Purchasing power per person 1993 U.S. dollars	7 Women's advancement 1993 Index (1= best)	8 Number of cars 1993 thousands	9 Number of letters and cards posted per person 1992	
605	200	71	25.0	–	Rwanda
401	7,780	54	2,675.0	21.54	Saudi Arabia
1,385	730	69	115.0	0.80	Senegal
201	6,370	–	–	40.61	Seychelles
830	140	100	47.7	0.24	Sierra Leone
275	19,310	21	435.0	108.25	Singapore
–	1,900	–	–	–	Slovak Republic
–	6,310	–	640.8	–	Slovenia
179	750	–	–	–	Solomon Islands
1,333	–	96	15.0	–	Somalia
–	2,900	43	5,108.3	–	South Africa
209	13,650	19	15,799.1	–	Spain
365	600	40	330.0	21.56	Sri Lanka
959	–	92	66.7	0.18	Sudan
112	1,210	–	–	–	Suriname
296	1,050	–	38.0	8.75	Swaziland
161	24,830	4	3,905.6	–	Sweden
93	36,410	8	3,409.1	–	Switzerland
920	–	50	360.0	0.84	Syria
96	470	–	13.8	–	Tajikistan
–	100	–	3,622.5	–	Taiwan
938	2,040	45	85.0	3.20	Tanzania
620	330	–	3,016.5	11.25	Thailand
686	1,610	82	37.5	–	Togo
201	3,730	22	203.6	10.95	Trinidad & Tobago
516	1,780	46	575.0	12.38	Tunisia
505	2,120	–	2,915.9	17.44	Turkey
92	1,380	–	–	–	Turkmenistan
1,248	190	83	43.1	0.55	Uganda
7	1,910	–	–	5.13	Ukraine
346	22,470	41	335.0	29.99	United Arab Emirates
160	17,970	9	26,838.7	298.12	United Kingdom
194	24,750	7	189,694.0	360.01	United States
221	3,910	29	425.0	2.92	Uruguay
83	960	–	–	–	Uzbekistan
385	2,840	–	1,981.8	3.62	Venezuela
261	170	30	124.5	–	Vietnam
–	–	–	–	–	Western Sahara
1,136	–	105	700.0	0.27	Yemen
–	–	–	3,700.0	–	Yugoslavia
701	–	85	180.0	–	Zaire
284	370	86	165.0	–	Zambia
1,959	540	56	225.0	–	Zimbabwe

...ternal mortality, infant mortality, life expectancy, post-secondary school enrolment, share of paid employment and participation in national parliament; ...l 8: Motor Industry of Great Britain, World Resources 1994-95; Col 9: Union Postale Universelle, Statistique des services postaux 1992.

NOTES

1 EXIT

'Human disturbance' is a measure of the threat to natural habitats and the life that depends on them. The World Resources Institute classifies human disturbance as high, medium or low. This map concentrates on what is defined as high human disturbance. But it should be interpreted with caution. Djibouti, for instance, does not appear on the map because both the high and low human disturbance in this state is zero; however, the medium human disturbance is 100 percent. These measures are given only for the proportion of the land area affected. Human disturbance at sea and along the coastline in particular can have a devastating effect directly or through the food chain. This is not recorded in the available sources.

The extinction of certain mammal and bird species is more than impoverishing in itself. It serves as an intimation of what may threaten all life on our planet, in the reckless pursuit of what is regarded as progress. Mammals and birds are not the only life forms with species in imminent danger of extinction. Many species of plants are disappearing, too.

2 MAYHEM

Some states, generally the rich ones, are taking measures to expand their forest cover, since trees take in carbon dioxide and give out oxygen in a natural process that serves to reduce the impact of the 'greenhouse' gases emitted elsewhere. Reforestation does not, however, prevent the same states from engaging in a timber trade which induces other states, generally the poor ones, to continue denuding their own forest cover. The same hypocrisy laments the growth in air pollution whilst at the same time encouraging the production and sale of fossil fuel driven vehicles which are a major cause of such pollution.

The evidence and implications of global warming are increasingly clear, not least to the insurance business, which has its own direct interest. In 1994, Frank Nutter, President of the Reinsurance Association of America, warned: 'The insurance business is first in line to be affected by climate change....it could bankrupt the industry.' But even long-complacent governments are becoming alarmed. A secret UK government report of 1990 revealed this in a warning that parts of the country would have to be abandoned in the event of sea-level rises.

Other forms of environmental mayhem are illustrated by major chemical incidents or accidents cited by the United Nations Environment Programme. These demonstrate an alarming readiness, in the interest of private profit or the supposed growth of the national economy, to take risks not just with the safety of particular communities but with the biosphere itself.

3 THE SCORCHERS

In the wake of the warmest November of the warmest year (1994) ever recorded, it is difficult to deny confidently that the world is heating up, particularly after our experience of the 1980s as the warmest decade ever. It is also difficult to reject the forecast by the United Nations Intergovernmental Panel on Climate Change, that – whatever measures we may take now – average global temperatures will have risen in 2030 by about 2°C above pre-industrial levels (1.1°C above 1995 levels) and by 2090 by 4°C (3.3°C above 1995. This would make the earth hotter than it has been for 120,000 years.

There is a strong connection between global warming and the buildup of greenhouse gases resulting from human activity. These gases are primarily made up of carbon dioxide arising from the use of fossil fuels, cement-making and deforestation; chlorofluorocarbons (which are mainly responsible for the depletion of the ozone layer) arising from refrigeration, the manufacture of solvents and foam products; and methane, from wet rice cultivation, factory farming and the production and transport of natural gas. Together these account for 86 percent of the human-generated greenhouse gases.

We are doing very little to restrain the buildup of greenhouse gases. Energy efficiency varies widely from country to country and, within countries, between users. International agreements to limit emissions are easier to sign than to enforce.Even an agreement on what to do is as difficult as the doing.

4 THE GUZZLERS

Energy is the feedstock of material abundance and personal choice. Hundreds of millions of people will suffer hunger, disease, discomfort and physical and mental confinement because they do not have access to enough of it. But if we continue to produce and consume energy in the quantities and in the ways we do now, even more people will suffer, perhaps terminally.

The dilemma might be avoided in part by using energy less prodigally. Just five percent as much energy is needed to recycle aluminium as to produce it from bauxite, the original raw material. For steel produced entirely from scrap, the savings amount roughly to two thirds. Newsprint from recycled paper takes 25-60 percent less energy to make than that from wood pulp. Recycling glass saves up to a third of the energy embodied in the original product.

The joule is a general measure of energy use, equivalent to 0.239 calories. One gigajoule equals one billion joules and is equivalent to 34.1 tonnes of coal or 23.8 tonnes of oil.

5 INFERNAL COMBUSTION

How good and yet how bad is the car. It is a device that enables us to move further and carry more than ever before, but hinders our access to where we want to be; that saves time, but dissipates it by extending the distances we travel; that covers ground, and buries it under tar or concrete; that enlarges personal freedom, and undermines the social connectedness that gives it meaning; that clears cities of refuse, and pollutes their atmosphere; that saves lives and maims them.

Directly and indirectly, the car is the most expensive means of transport in use: in air pollution costs, it is sixteen times more expensive than trains, twice as much as planes; in CO_2 emissions, the car costs twice as much as trains (although half that of planes); in noise pollution, it is four times as costly as trains (although less by a quarter as noisy as planes). Cars are respectively ten times and 69 times more costly in accidents than trains and planes. Altogether, the external costs of motor passenger transport are 725 percent higher than transport by train, and 190 percent higher than transport by air.

This does not stop governments from continuing to encourage car ownership and to invest in road building rather than in public transport systems.

6 URBAN BLIGHT

Shrinking economic opportunities in rural areas and the lure of enhanced opportunities and services in cities combine to promote a process of urbanization that is all but ubiquitous. Furthermore, the process is accelerating. From 1875 to 1900, the annual rate of urban growth in the rich world was 2.8 percent. In the poor world, urban populations grew at an annual rate of around 4 percent from 1975 to 1990. On present trends, half the world's population will be urbanized by the year 2005, and two thirds by the year 2025. By the year 2025, some 4 billion people in developing countries will be classified as urban, equivalent to the world's total population in 1975.

For all the advantages in employment, education and access to medical care that may benefit many people in urban areas, the environmental impact of the megacities is likely to be formidable. City residents tend to consume more industrial goods and energy-intensive services, especially in developing countries, and urban populations everywhere create concentrated air pollution, water pollution and solid waste.

7 MULTIPLICATION

China's 'floating population' of illegal city dwellers numbers 100 million or more; and the population of hidden 'black babies', born despite the official one child family policy, must be counted in the tens of millions. Elsewhere population censuses are the outcome of politics rather than their shapers; in Nigeria or Lebanon, for example, where censuses are routinely rigged or avoided, and even in the stable, rich countries whenever constituencies are adjusted to take account of demographic changes. There are isolated, marginal people everywhere: hostiles, illegals, anti-socials and a-socials, who have cause to avoid officialdom. And there are innumerate census enumerators, often engaged in more pressing business, who prefer the cool of their office to the heat and possible danger of the world outside.

If it were not for the international agencies, such as the Population Division of the United Nations, we would hardly know how many we are, where we are, and how fast our number is growing. They provide annual estimates of all states' populations and an essential critique of the often self-serving national figures. However, even UN figures, particularly its forecasts, should be treated with caution. Reproduction habits can change unexpectedly; wars can deplete and disperse whole populations; mass migrations can swarm suddenly. At the end of the 1980s, no fewer than six states – Afghanistan, Angola, Cambodia, Chad, Laos and Nicaragua – were thought to have less than 90 percent of the population that had been predicted for them at the beginning of that decade.

The population projections in the map are based on reasonable assumptions about the future course of fertility, mortality and migration. They do not allow for sudden eruptions of war, natural disasters or unexpected changes in disease patterns.

States with under 0.05 percent of the world's population – less than 2.75 million today and 4.21 in 2025 – do not feature in the cartogram. There are 53 of these, and their combined population in mid-1993 was 47 million.

8 DIASPORAS

People do not always stay in the countries or even the continents where they were born. Some go, or are taken, in large numbers elsewhere in the world. These are the origins of diasporas.

As widely differing estimates for the black components in the populations of Brazil, Cuba and Colombia indicate, the extent of the black diaspora is nowhere more difficult to establish than in an agreed classification of who is black. Despite colour distinctions within the black community of the U.S.A., blacks are defined there, not least by themselves, as people of part or whole African ancestry. In Brazil, where people define themselves, for the purposes of the census, as white, yellow, red, brown or black, the bias is strongly towards levitation as far up the scale of prevailing racial value as credibility suggests, and often further. In Cuba, where the government has long regarded racial identity as a domestic distraction when not a political deviation, official census returns have remained undisclosed and are likely to be unreliable. We have chosen to use the U.S. demographic definition and to rely on such expert estimates as are available. In general, the higher estimates are likely to be the more valid ones.

We have not included in the map on the black diaspora every country outside Africa where any blacks live, since this would scarcely be of much relevance or value. Where the black component of the population is below one percent, we have identified only those countries with still substantial communities or where there is, however small the communities, some evidence of related social tension. Blacks are all too often a prime target of white racism, and discrimination against them takes numerous forms. We have given examples of functional segregation in the U.S.A., but it is widespread in other countries, such as the UK, too. Despite traditional and official pretences to the contrary, for instance, Brazilian society is profoundly racist, but the information on functional segregation is not available to illustrate it here.

The Indian diaspora also provides difficulties of demographic definition, though for different reasons. The India of the British Raj, from which so many indentured labourers were drawn, became with independence the states of India and Pakistan, and Pakistan subsequently became the two states of Pakistan and Bangladesh. For most countries, we have defined Indians as members of communities which originated from the Indian sub-continent, since separation of them into Indians, Pakistanis and Bangladeshis is not possible and would make no historical sense. Where official statistics make the relevant distinction, as in the UK where such settlement is overwhelmingly recent, we use only those for Indians. For Pakistan and Bangladesh themselves, we use the definition of Hindus.

The Chinese diaspora produces no such difficulties. It has been chosen, rather than the Armenian or Greek diasporas, for instance, since it is, like the black and Indian diasporas, a target of hostility and discrimination in certain societies.

9 THE QUANTITY OF LIFE

Living long and living well are not the same. This map concentrates on physical survival and the conditions that make it possible, primarily safe water and adequate health care. What it feels like to be alive is shown in the following map (The Quality of Life).

The indicators we have for both maps are horribly crude. Take health care, for instance. It can be safely assumed that almost everyone in the U.S.A. could, if need be, reach a medical facility within an hour using normal means of transport – the conventional criterion of access to care. Yet there are between 31 and 37 million Americans who are not covered by medical insurance, and many more who are underinsured, and so effectively denied medical attention. In theory, all Russian citizens are covered by medical insurance; in practice, some of the treatment on offer is so poor and the facilities so unhygienic that they are avoided at all costs.

Over-aggregation (the loss of relevant detail in making broad categories) affects this map, and the one following, in other ways. Life expectancy at birth – the basic ingredient of the main map – takes no account of the fact that women generally live significantly longer than men. The data on access to safe water conceals the enormous differences in provision between rural and urban areas in a bland, often meaningless, national average.

Over-aggregation is not the only, or indeed, the most grievous of the data's sins. Simply, they contain too many round fractions – halves, thirds, quarters – to inspire confidence. They reek of the office and of written records, not of the real world with all its particularities. But they are the best we have and approximate reality even if they do not represent it accurately.

10 THE QUALITY OF LIFE

If people were allowed to move about freely, we might learn a great deal about how they experience life in different places. Since they are not, we have to make do with conjecture and with measurements that rest on the wobbliest of assumptions, namely, that what makes for happiness – or misery, as the case may be – is more or less the same everywhere; that people can increase the one, or avoid the other, through personal commitment and political will; that meaningful comparisons can be made between one person and another, and between one society and another.

These assumptions reveal more about the measurer than the measured. They reflect a view of people as social, mutually supportive creatures and a view of world society as essentially a unity marred occasionally by conflict, not a disparity occasionally drawn together in harmony. It is a view held by a relatively small circle of privileged, Western-educated intellectuals steeped in world affairs – a humane, optimistic view with which, broadly, this atlas agrees. But it is not a majority view, and the indicators of human fulfilment or development that it propounds are not objective.

The Human Development Index compiled by the United Nations Development Programme is the most ambitious of its type. It combines life expectancy at birth (between 25 and 85 years), adult literacy (0 to 100 percent), years of schooling (between 0 and 15) and real income (between 200 and 40,000 'international' dollars of equal purchasing power).

Some of the indicators it uses are weak because they rest on statistical sand; some because of the nature of the evidence; some because of the way that evidence is gathered. All suffer because they rest on national averages, as if there were, or could be, an average human experience.

The inset map and graphic illustrate harder evidence for the stresses of life in the contemporary world: the needless shortening of its span, despite the miracles of modern medicine, and its undervaluation.

11 RICH AND POOR

1.3 billion people cannot afford a nutritionally-adequate diet and essential non-food requirements; they live in absolute poverty. On the other hand, there are 223 billionaire families who live in absolute riches, scarcely able to consume personally the interest on the interest from their investments.

Of the 53 countries for which comparable estimates exist, Botswana and Brazil, half way down the list in average income per head (23rd and 28th respectively), nonetheless top the bill in income inequality; Sweden, Norway and the Netherlands (7th, 11th and 15th respectively in average income per head) show as much inequality as Ethiopia or Uganda, the two poorest in average income per head.

12 BREADLINES

The availability of adequate nourishment in a particular state is not the same as adequate provision for all of its inhabitants. Nor do calories themselves guarantee health. Other constituents of a diet, such as adequate protein and vitamins, are necessary. To take only one example, Mexico has available 131 percent of the average calorie need, yet 14 percent of its children under the age of five are estimated to suffer from malnutrition, and the growth of 22 percent of those aged from 24 to 59 months is stunted.

Statistics for available average calories are duly listed for the rich countries, which do not provide estimates for the incidence of malnutrition and stunting among children. Such absences from the statistics do not necessarily match reality. In some rich countries, such as the U.S.A. and UK, the incidence of poverty and deprivation is not only widespread but rising.

13 CONNECTIONS

In 1965, 85 percent of the world's 150 million telephone lines were in Europe and North America. Fax was almost unknown and computer networking a contradiction in terms. There was just one trans-Atlantic telephone cable which could handle 89 calls at a time, and a handful of radio links across the Pacific. 'Mobile' telephones were unknown. A three minute phone call from the U.S.A. to Europe or Asia (assuming you could get through) cost, typically, U.S. $90 at 1995 prices (U.S. $18 at the time) and much more if the call were made in the other direction.

In 1995 the global network comprised more than 600 million telephone lines and over 1.2 billion terminals in some 190 countries. There were faxes galore, computer networks travelling into information highways, and ever proliferating 'mobiles'. The cable and satellite network across the Atlantic handled almost a million simultaneous calls at between U.S. $1 and $1.50 per minute from Europe, and half that price from the U.S.A. Satellite communications now cover the world.

You might say that a great deal has changed in one generation. But not that much – as yet. CNN, the satellite-distributed news network, and Internet, the transnational matrix of computer networks, together reach no more than two percent of the world's population. The rest are dependent on 'snail mail' – the postal system – as the mainstay of their contacts beyond the narrow horizons of face-to-face, local communication and personal travel. In 1991 the average amount of time spent on international calls per year – about seven minutes – straddled a huge range, from seven hours per citizen in Luxembourg to six seconds in Africa.

14 ILLITERACY

Many states neglect to record the problem of illiteracy in their midst and others underestimate the number of illiterate adults in the population. For this map, therefore, we have had to rely on estimates, supplied by UNESCO and the CIA. UNESCO records nothing more precise than an illiteracy rate of below five percent in advanced industrial states.

Symbols on the map illustrate the ratio of female to male illiteracy. Most of the recent statistics available demonstrate that the difference between the proportions of illiterate men and women is marked and sometimes enormous. However, recent statistics are simply not available for many of the industrialized states. Only Greece, Italy, Portugal and Spain provide relevant statistics for as late as 1990. Those provided for Belgium, France and the U.S.A., as for Bulgaria, Hungary and Romania, date back to 1970. There are no relevant statistics available for the successor states of either the USSR or Yugoslavia, and the statistics we have used belong to these states before their break-up. Those for Yugoslavia, at least, date back to only 1990. Those for the USSR date back to 1970.

15 WASTING LIVES

The high rates of mortality among the children of the poor represent a hideous and unpardonable waste of human life. Nor is that by any means the only such waste. For many, mere survival is, in another sense, a deadend. Children who survive are often deprived of the education that might otherwise enable them to realize their potential. As adults, they are often relegated to the edges of the economy, where their lives are at risk from their inability to earn an adequate wage.

16 MISSING WOMEN

By law or convention, all but a very few women are denied control over the productive assets that lend economic independence. In some (poor and not so poor) countries where land is particularly important in sustaining life they are denied ownership rights to it, or equal ownership rights with men. In others, even some of the richest states, they are denied finance through mortgage-lending or banking policies which are defined in a way that assumes men to be the dominant economic agents and thus perpetuates the status quo. In Iran, for instance, a widow inherits a mere eighth of her husband's estate; a daughter gets one share for every two inherited by her brother. From that primordial denial flows a secondary denial – of education – and a tertiary one – of influential, well-paid work.

There is a substantial body of data on women's share of education, of certain jobs, of the market in consuming this or that, but not of women's share in the ownership and control of productive assets. Nobody really knows much about discrimination in access to productive property. There are, as yet, no universally agreed indicators, let alone any serious attempts to measure its incidence worldwide. The United Nations Development Programme promises to address this gap in our knowledge in its Human Development Report for 1995. Meanwhile, and long after that is published, women will continue to work twice as hard as men for half or less in paid income; will continue to have unwanted babies, usually the only dependable source of additional labour and income (in poor countries), and of status, pride and spiritual nourishment (in all countries).

The cumulative result of discrimination and social impotence is that there are far fewer women than there would be in a more even-handed world. In some countries, such as China, many female babies are simply killed at birth; in others, such as India, many are overworked, undernourished and neglected to destruction. The number of 'missing women' is the difference between the number of females in a population and the number who would be alive if they retained their natural female to male ratio at birth (94.6:100).

17 BODY POLITICS

The battle lines between the private, creative and caring realm of parenting and the public, impersonal, instrumental world of population policies and state interest run through the very centre of women's bodies. The outcome of that battle is in constant flux: sometimes, when labour is scarce as in the rich states in the 1960s, women find it possible, although never easy, to extend the frontiers of control over their bodies. In times of recession and idleness, women find such frontiers contracting. Nowhere is this more apparent than in Eastern Europe where the collapse of Communism, profligate with labour as with so many other things, has meant a sharp turnabout in what were once among the most liberal abortion regimes in the world. The personal has paid heavily for the political in those countries.

The law on abortion does not everywhere reflect clinical practice. In most Muslim states, and in many Latin American and African ones, the law is more liberal than the reality; while in Israel, New Zealand and South Africa, legal abortion rates approach those in states which permit abortion on demand. Interpretations of the same law can vary widely within a state, as in Switzerland. In some ostensibly restrictive states – Bangladesh for example – menstrual regulation, that is, early abortion without a pregnancy test, is freely available; whereas in some ostensibly liberal states – Togo, for example – legal abortions are few in number because the services are scarce or not available.

The worldwide trend towards liberalism in abortion law since the 1960s is, for these reasons, more a matter of ideology and political rhetoric than of women's experience. It might well be that the institutionalization of medicine and its embrace of pregnancy and childbirth, have widened women's choices in theory while narrowing them in practice.

Abortion is one method of exercising control over childbirth. Less extreme, although almost as politically charged, is the accessibility of birth control and the range of choices available.

Domestic violence is often unacknowledged and frequently concealed. The victims as well as the perpetrators may go to great lengths to hide evidence of wife-beating and marital rape, so records are haphazard and scarcely scientific.

18 CHILD EXPLOITATION

The most widespread form of abusing children is almost certainly their employment, sometimes below the age of six, as workers. Yet here, as with other forms of child abuse, information is scarce and often merely indicative. An ILO (International Labour Office) study has been undertaken, but information on a national basis is not yet available. The statutory provisions for minimum age requirements, themselves all too often more honoured in the breach than the observance, nonetheless say much of the way children are treated in numerous states. The currently most detailed source is the U.S. State Department's Country Reports on Human Rights Practices. Particular studies of child labour, most disturbing in their details, come from the International Confederation of Free Trade Unions.

The 1989 United Nations' Convention on the Rights of the Child sets out to promote the basic health care and education of the young, as well as their protection from abuse, exploitation or neglect, at home, at work, and in armed conflicts. A recent report on 'The Progress of Nations', from UNICEF (United Nations Children's Fund), testifies to the readiness of governments to sign the Convention, without a commensurate readiness to ratify their adherence or comply with their undertakings. The sexual exploitation of children by foreigners, evidently condoned or inadequately suppressed by most governments, is the subject of one study in the UNICEF report; the incidence of infant deaths from presumed abuse, which highlights the difference between the U.S.A. and Denmark at one extreme and Italy and Spain at the other, the subject of another. In each case, the information covers only selected states, and others are not to be presumed innocent because they are not included.

19 THE KILLING WEED

Half a million Americans are hooked on heroin, 3 million are regular users of cocaine and crack, and 15 million are alcoholics or alcohol-dependants. This is the official count in 1995. Unofficial estimates run three times higher. Taking the unofficial count and adding to it the untold addicts of all the other natural and artificial mood modifiers would still not bring us anywhere near the number of nicotine addicts – perhaps 53 million – spending U.S. $60 billion a year, including taxes, on their habit and probably costing as much again in health care and accidental damage. By contrast, illicit drug use of all sorts is estimated to cost some U.S. $30 billion a year.

The comparison between nicotine and other drugs is as dramatic elsewhere. In the Netherlands, cigarette smoking is reckoned to cause nine times as many deaths as all other addictions. In the UK more than twice the number of deaths are attributable to cigarette-smoking as to self-administered barbiturate poisoning plus alcohol.

Consumers are locked into tobacco's addictive qualities, business into its dependable cash flow, government into its taxability. Nicotine addiction is a public addiction and, for that reason, appears – wrongly – less harmful than its more private, often illegal, competitors. It is a domesticated addiction, not generally linked to crime or violence, so that it appears – wrongly – more acceptable socially. Like all addictions, it appears to offer a sanctuary from stress and failure. It does not.

In the U.S.A. the proportion of adults smoking has dropped from 42 percent to 26 percent since 1955. Almost 90 percent of Americans – including a third of all smokers – tell pollsters they find cigarette smoke annoying. The number supporting a total ban on smoking indoors, as opposed to milder measures such as the installation of no-smoking areas, has nearly doubled since 1983, to 35 percent. Since 1986 the proportion of firms that has banned smoking on their premises has risen from 2 percent to 34 percent. In 1993, the Environmental Protection Agency officially classified secondhand smoke as a health hazard.

With sales of U.S. $45 billion a year, the American tobacco giants are still profitable and powerful. But they are less confident than they have been in the past. For although their sales in Asia and Eastern Europe are expected to explode, the new markets are unlikely to be as profitable in the short run as the domestic market. And in the long run they might well catch the American virus of health consciousness and care.

20 PLAGUES NEW AND RENEWED

The spread of AIDS has been gathering pace, not least in countries where the rates were previously low. In its report of July 1994 on 'The Current Global Situation of the HIV/AIDS Pandemic', the World Health Organisation (WHO) declared: 'Allowing for under-diagnosis, incomplete reporting, and reporting delay, and based on the available data on HIV infections around the world, it is estimated that around 4 million AIDS cases in adults and children have occurred worldwide since the pandemic began'. This represents a 60 percent increase over the estimated 2.5 million cases as of July 1993 or only one year before. The map gives national totals of reported AIDS cases, where these exceed 10,000, up to the end of March 1994. Corresponding totals for the end of 1990, with the percentage increase from then up to March 1994, reveal how rapid and sometimes explosive the rate of increase has been: Brazil 20,578 (140%); Côte d'Ivoire 6,898 (171%); Kenya 15,252 (948%); Malawi 14,851 (115%); Mexico 5,905 (211%); Rwanda 4,489 (138%); Spain 7,304 (231%); Tanzania 22,081 (75%); Uganda 19,955 (120%); U.S.A. 190,774 (116%); Zaire 16,147 (41%); Zambia 4,202 (608%); and Zimbabwe 5,994 (366%).

Tuberculosis was supposed to be in retreat from improving social conditions and the development of new drugs by advances in medicine. Yet, while the incidence may be declining in some states today, it is rising – often sharply – in others. As with diphtheria, another disease emerging as a serious scourge again, this is related to deteriorating social conditions, in poor countries or among the poor within rich ones. In March 1995, the World Health Organisation predicted that tuberculosis will kill at least 30 million people over the next decade and could infect some two billion, or more than a third of the world's population. In particular, it warned that unless remedial action was taken within three years, tuberculosis would assume catastrophic proportions in many of the successor states of the former USSR.

21 WANTED HANDS

The labour force is conventionally divided among three categories of economic activity. Agriculture includes hunting, fishing and forestry as well as farming. Industry includes mining, construction, water, gas and electricity, as well as manufacturing. Services account for the rest, such as wholesale and retail trading; restaurants and hotels; transport and communications; finance, insurance, real estate and other business services, as well as social and personal ones.

A high proportion of employment in agriculture is generally an indication of economic backwardness and poverty. A high proportion in industry, however, is not a sure sign of corresponding economic advancement. Some of the highest proportions are in Eastern European states and successor states of the former USSR where productivity is low, and what is produced is not always marketable. A high proportion of employment in services is often taken as a more reliable guide to economic advancement, but the correlation is not invariable. At one extreme, such employment may reflect a substantial sector of involvement in finance and insurance, information technology and telecommunications; at another it may merely reflect a substantial dependence on tourism or a disproportionate government bureaucracy.

22 VALUE SUBTRACTED

The term 'exploitation' has largely disappeared from the vocabulary of current politics. This does not, however, make the fact of exploitation any less real. And whatever it may be called, its existence is implicitly recognized by the measure of 'earnings as percentage of value added' (value added being what is charged for the product after deduction of material costs) in the World Bank's information on 'manufacturing activity'.

The rates of exploitation which the paucity of relevant statistics allows do not coincide with the differentials between rich and poor countries. Niger is at one extreme and the Central African Republic at the other, for instance. In both cases, the size of the manufacturing sector in relation to the economy is so small that quirks may be responsible for the differential. Regrettably there are no relevant statistics for the successor states of the former USSR. Yet, for all of the reservations we have about the data on which the map is based, the information it contains remains useful, and illustrative of the phenomenon with which it deals.

23 THE LABOUR FORCE

The right of workers to combine in advancing their own interests against the power and exactions of their employers was dearly bought and was a crucial contribution to the advance of democracy itself. It is a right that lost none of its meaning for being abused, as it was in the former USSR, and other one-party states, which made trade unionism an important component in securing the obedience of labour and its service to the regime. Even in the traditional democracies trade unions have not always been innocent of abusing democracy itself, as officials have gained or perpetuated control by manipulating election.

Yet the right remains more important than its abuse, and has in recent years been notably asserted by trade unions in the cause of democratizing their societies. Trade unions were central, for instance, to the defeat of the authoritarian regime in Poland, as in other states of the former Soviet system. In Latin America, especially in Argentina, Bolivia, Brazil, Chile, Ecuador, Peru and Uruguay, unions were crucial in the popular and eventually successful challenge to repressive regimes. The same has been true in Africa. Revolt against one party regimes in Congo, Mali, Niger and Zambia has been led by trade unions. Even as these notes are being written, trade unions in Nigeria are challenging military rule. In other states, trade unions are asserting their independence.

It is scarcely surprising that in a number of countries where monarchical, theocratic or other forms of unelected rule do not encumber themselves with even the pretensions to democracy, trade unions are banned altogether or allowed to exist only in conditions of the closest government control. Yet trade unions are also under attack in parts of the avowedly democratic and industrially advanced world. Recent legislation in the UK, for example, on the pretext of dealing with trade union abuses, has abridged their rights as well, and membership has declined steeply. There, and in other states, this decline in trade union membership is partly due to the economic shift from industry, the traditional home of trade unionism, to the service sector, but it is also due to a rising rate of unemployment, which has encouraged employers to be more exacting in their requirements. Employers become more determined to hire only non-unionized labour, and workers more willing to accept this condition. There is a clear connection, for instance, between the decline of union membership in the U.S.A., from 30 percent of the workforce in the mid-1960s to 16 percent in the mid-1990s, and the fact that in 1991 unionized workers there were paid on average 23 percent more than those in non-unionized enterprises.

In other democratic states, however, and in those which are enjoying industrial success, such as South Korea, trade union membership has been rising rapidly.

Statistics on strikes and lock-outs are available only for a relatively few countries. We have included such information, however, to illustrate continuing labour militancy and the varying rates of this from one country to another.

24 WOMEN IN WORK

Statistics for the participation of women in the labour force must be treated with caution, especially those for the poorer countries. Women frequently work in the informal sector of the economy, selling food and trading in household goods, or in unregulated industries and services, where their activity goes largely unrecorded. In poorer countries, their work as subsistence labour in agriculture is all too often assigned little or no economic value by governments and ignored in labour statistics. In Pakistan, for instance, such statistics exclude an estimated 12 million agricultural workers. Domestic labour outside the home is similarly disregarded, even though collecting and transporting food and water, for example, are essential activities which may require several hours of work each day.

In theory, the proportion of women in parliament should advance in step with democracy. In South Africa, the first democratic election, in April 1994, raised the proportion from 3 percent to 25 percent. This is an unusual correspondence, however, as is all too clear from the low proportions of women in parliament in such long lived democracies as those of France, the UK and the U.S.A. Real democracy has yet to surmount the gender issue.

25 UNEMPLOYMENT

The officially high rates for unemployment in most of the advanced industrial states, where governments were not so long ago committed to objectives of full employment, are socially wasteful and unsettling enough. But the real rates may well be significantly higher than the recorded figures suggest. The rate of unemployment is a sensitive political issue, and the official figures record only those officially defined as unemployed. In the UK, for instance, such definitions have been frequently revised, and a substantial number of the unemployed may be concealed in other categories such as that for recipients of invalidity benefits. In some advanced industrial states, unemployment is a term applied only to job-seekers, and unemployment benefits are paid only for a stipulated period. In such circumstances, unrecorded numbers of the unemployed may stop seeking jobs after repeated experiences of failure and may simply rely on basic social benefits.

Statistics for the successor states of the USSR are not so much manipulated as irrelevant, since many of the supposedly employed are in state enterprises which function fitfully and pay wages that consign their employees to poverty, if not destitution. Figures for many poor countries are either unavailable or apply only to a relatively small sector of the economy, to the urban areas, or only to the capital city. The figures for the rate of underemployment, applied to those people who work in casual, part-time or seasonal jobs, are more significant even though they are usually no more than estimates. Where there are specific reports and/or estimates, we have identified states with high levels of underemployment but these are by no means the only ones.

In a number of poor countries, figures for unemployment and underemployment would be much greater, were it not that many in the workforce are working abroad. In 1988, for instance, two and a half million Egyptians, equivalent to one sixth of that country's workforce, were estimated to be working abroad, most of them in Saudi Arabia and the Gulf states. At any one time, some 60 percent of the active male labour force in Lesotho are working in South Africa. Relatedly, figures for the net migration rate in 1993 are merely illustrative and partly deceptive. Migrants who leave may be balanced by migrants who return, on visits or at the end of employment contracts. For countries such as Egypt, the limits of labour recruitment abroad may well have been reached, as traditional recipients tighten their immigration policies.

26 A GLOBAL GRASP

The combined foreign sales power of the world's 100 top transnational corporations (TNCs) represent well over 40 percent of the world's total export trade. This is not the full extent of the TNCs' power. They can and often do have a marked impact, through the policy decisions they make, on the economies and politics of states. Except for a small minority in the state sector of the countries where they are domiciled, TNCs are effectively their own masters, answerable only to their shareholders. Since in almost all cases the shareholdings are widely diffused, this amounts to their being answerable only to themselves in the shape of their management boards.

In 1991, almost half (48.4 percent) of all sales by the 100 top TNCs came from countries other than their own, and well over a third (37.8 percent) of their total assets were held abroad. Foreign direct investment by TNCs totalled over U.S. $148 billion, and by far the bulk of such investment – almost U.S. $108 billion – went to the already developed economies. In the main, therefore, the TNCs invest in one another's backyards. While France, for instance, attracted U.S. $15.2 billion and the UK, U.S. $21.5 billion in 1991, China attracted only U.S. $4.4 billion and India a mere U.S. $961 million.

27 HEDGES AND BETS

Investment and speculation are as old as markets themselves. It has long been possible to buy shares on the stock exchange by contracting to pay for them at some stipulated future date or by trading in them on the basis of a 'margin', or backing, through the provision of cash or shares to meet a stipulated proportion – say, ten percent – of the value. It was essentially this 'margin' trading, on the great 'bull' or rising market in the late 1920s, that turned the fall on Wall Street in 1929 into a collapse, as 'margins' disappeared and the shares that provided them were sold to cover commitments. It has also long been possible to speculate similarly in the hope of a 'bear' or falling market, by selling shares without owning them, on the basis that they can be bought more cheaply later with a corresponding profit. The consequence of misjudgement or misfortune can be no less calamitous in this exercise. And what is done with shares can be done also with commodities, from copper and oil to pork bellies and frozen orange juice.

Increasingly, moreover, as financial markets have become more sophisticated, they have developed numerous new instruments, which may be used to hedge against risk but also to increase it. It is now possible to speculate not only on the future value of particular shares and commodities, but on future movements in the value of various currencies, interest rates, one or other stock market index, and in options or rights to undertake such transactions at a stipulated price by a stipulated date. On this basis, for instance, share prices can often be affected less by investment considerations than by speculative positions on the future movement of the stock exchange index.

The growing dominance of these so-called derivatives is being accompanied by growing disquiet among those responsible for financial regulation. The global nature and complexity of the derivative markets involve so many interlocking players that the risk is real of one financial collapse setting off others in an uncontainable series, whatever the underlying state of the real economy. When an oil company in Japan can lose U.S. $1.5 billion in trading foreign exchange derivatives, a German industrial company a similar sum by betting on movements in the oil market, and a U.S. soap and detergent firm over U.S. $100 million on interest rate derivatives, the question is whether the scale of speculation has not begun to dwarf that of investment.

As this book was going to press, Baring Brothers, the blue-blooded British merchant bank, collapsed after losses – estimated at close to £1 billion – in Japanese stock market index derivatives.

28 THE GOLDEN FIX

In October 1994, officials and ministers from more than 120 states gathered in Naples for a United Nations conference on organized international crime. Little came of it, of course. For however sincere individual representatives might have been about wanting to collaborate with one another, they were hampered by a combination of political rivalries, jealously guarded national legal systems, official corruption and sheer incompetence. And, as likely as not, they had been pre-empted by representatives of the new style multinational criminal corporations meeting in a hotel somewhere, in Eastern Europe perhaps.

These criminals are not cast in the mould of Al Capone, a near illiterate who acquired millions and did not know how to dispose of them, who wore flash suits and cashmere coats, who used naked fists and guns hidden in violin cases to get to the top, and who died of syphilis and paresis of the brain. The new hoods are cosmopolitan businessmen, well-educated, well-spoken, who know how to move among politicians and officials and transfer money from Wall Street to London to Paris and beyond. They are privileged people, with plenty of opportunities. They are just more than usually greedy as businessmen and so tempted to take the criminal route.

The profits accruing to them are huge. Pablo Escobar, the drug baron shot dead in late 1993 by the Colombian army with support from the CIA, the U.S. air force and the U.S. drug enforcement agency, is reputed to have authorized payments of U.S. $1 million per day to keep himself out of jail. More must have gone in bribes to keep open trade channels, to launder the proceeds of trade, and in investing in legitimate business. For the aim of the people who direct criminal multinationals is to drop the adjective – every generation has its robber barons eager to become merely barons.

They are willing to pay heavily for it. Members of the Cali cocaine cartel in Colombia, are reputed to pay 17-20 percent for money laundering services; and money brokers are often able to buy cash at a discount of 23 percent. The laundered money finds its way into lifestyle and cash-intensive industries – travel agencies, exchange houses, casinos and other gambling joints, international trading firms – as well as commercial and residential buildings and construction.

It is difficult to paint a dispassionate picture of criminal business. Business generally is secretive; criminal business, however defined (and that is an arbitrary matter) is even more so.

The best available source we have – the U.S. Bureau of International Narcotics Matters – is not without bias. It considers domestic drug consumption and indigenous supply less important than foreign supply and shipment to the U.S.; it values foreign collaboration with the U.S. authorities more highly than foreign action; it paints a better picture of countries favoured for other reasons such as Israel, and reports badly on countries out of favour, such as Cuba.

29 PRIVATIZATION

Privatization is for citizens a second expropriation by the state; the first is the taxation which paid for the assets in the first place.

For the purchasing companies, privatization is a quick, seemingly safe, route to increased profit, presence and power. For the divesting states, the motives are more complex. Some see it primarily as a necessary adjustment to the need for international economic mobility and to greater competition in the global market. Others see in privatization a way to relieve budgetary stress. Yet others use it to keep rich, foreign uncles from meddling in what they consider to be their internal affairs. And others use privatization to spread the charms of possession beyond the political class, and so to widen its base of support.

None of these aims is pursued to the exclusion of the others. Nor are they pursued with clinical purity. The advantages to be gained from breaking up state monopolies are often lost by conniving at or condoning private ones. Attempts to furnish or replenish Treasury coffers are qualified by giveaway prices for the aspiring privilegentsia.

Even assuming that the aim of privatization is clear and uncorrupted, there are natural limits to it everywhere except in the heartlands of the market system. The state has built its business – badly in most cases, madly in some – where the domestic private sector proved unequal to the task of fending off or challenging foreign economic might. The state commandeered enormous resources in the process, further weakening, where it did not extinguish, private enterprise. Now that the major state commercial bodies are seen to be at best awkward players in world markets, or at worst, clear losers, there is usually no one left on whom to unload them except – cruel irony – the foreign private enterprises they were designed to resist in the first place.

In brief, privatization is a primrose path to an unprecedented concentration of economic power in ever-fewer, ever-larger hands on a world scale, and to its equal and opposite – an unprecedented loss of economic power by an ever-larger number.

30 MUFFLED VOICES

The different categories we employ for this map are our own, chosen to define general distinctions among so many particular ones, and to provide some basic historical perspective.

The term 'established multi-party democratic system' implies no comment on the content of the democracy involved. Any category that encompasses Sweden, Senegal and Guatemala is necessarily broad. All that is implied is that a multi-party political system, with elections by supposedly secret ballot on a basis of adult suffrage, has traditionally, if not always continuously, been in place. Where appropriate, certain qualifications have been added, such as interruptions by periods of military rule or the significant incidence of extra-judicial violence as a form of political pressure. The second term, 'recently adopted multi-party democratic system, or in transition to one', identifies states, most notably those that were formerly part of the USSR, which have emerged from a recent past of one-party regimes or, as in the case of South Africa, some other kind of developed repressive rule. The term 'one-party regime' is also broad. It encompasses not only states where this system is constitutionally sustained but also those, such as Mexico and Kenya, where ballot rigging, intimidation, and/or institutional structures of control have secured a one-party regime in fact, if not in form. Terms for the remaining categories require no elaboration.

31 NOTIONAL INCOME

Gross National Product (GNP) and Gross Domestic Product (GDP) are the most widely-used general measures of economic power, and for that reason alone are unavoidable when making international comparisons. They measure the consumption of goods and services that are bought or paid for in taxes. They do not normally count unmarketed goods produced for home consumption, and do not include at all the untraded services, from sex to socialization, which are essential for human life. They therefore underrate the incomes of rural and family-oriented societies and exaggerate those of industrial ones and of societies resting on nuclear and sub-nuclear families. They do not cover the cost, in depletion and damage, of economic activity and, therefore, understate the incomes of traditional and subsistence-agriculture societies where such exist, and overstate those of resource-based, market-oriented economies. They do not distinguish between productive and unproductive activity – between making butter and making guns – and, therefore, confuse economic with military power, in the short term at least. In consequence, whatever their virtues as pointers to the current resources available or potentially available to the state, they are inadequate yardsticks of human welfare or social health.

Even within its own terms, national accounting is flawed. It is insensitive to changes in consumption patterns, and so an imperfect guide to recent changes. Expressed in a single national currency – conventionally, the U.S. dollar – national accounting is at the mercy of exchange rates which can and often do gyrate madly.

A different measure, developed by the UN's International Comparison Project, is 'real' GDP, based on purchasing power. This attempts to gauge what countries – or individuals – could buy if they shopped in a single world supermarket.

'Real' GDP is better than the conventional measure in that it makes allowance for different cost structures. A medical consultation is a medical consultation anywhere in the world, but it is more expensive compared to a hamburger in the U.S.A. than it is compared to a chapatti in India. The same is true generally of services in comparison with manufactures.

'Real' GDP shares many problems with its conventional cousin: the difficulty of conversion into a standard measure (in this case 'international dollars'); weaknesses in accounting for goods and services not normally traded commercially; insensitivity to the effects of economic activity on the environment. But it does put right some of the distortions engendered by that cousin, and it shows, in broad outline, that world purchasing power, although still shockingly concentrated in a few states, is more evenly spread amongst them than world income.

32 FIRST CHARGE

Saddam Hussein is building the world's biggest mosque in Baghdad, capital city of war-ravaged, starving Iraq. Pakistan, one of the poorest of states, is spending untold billions on nuclear weapons.

Governments worldwide, be they autocratic or democratic, spend vast sums on objects or projects of their desire, not of their citizens' choice. They spend money in our name, largely unconstrained by our wishes. A nuclear power station here, a major road through unspoilt country there, an airport in the bush or a seaport on the rocks. Worldwide, one quarter of the U.S.$7 trillion they spend goes on paying their own salaries, and another tenth on keeping their military forces fed, housed and armed, compared with just over a tenth on health or education.

33 FOOD POWER

National self-sufficiency in food production is not a sign of an adequate diet or even of freedom from hunger, but it is a pre-condition for them.

As Earl Butz, a combative U.S. Agricultural Secretary, once said in the 1980s, 'Food is a weapon. It is now one of the principal weapons in our negotiating kit'. As a weapon, it is used by big and small alike, at home (in Sudan, for example) and abroad (by the U.S. or the European Union).

It is a weapon few states are likely to lay down. Although average agricultural yields differ wildly from state to state – from 6,650 kilograms of cereal per hectare in the Netherlands to 380 in Angola in the late 1980s – which leaves plenty of room for improvement in the world as a whole. No conceivable growth in productivity, even coupled with an extension of land available for food crops, will make all states self-sufficient within their current borders.

34 INDUSTRIAL POWER

The latest statistics available have not caught up with the breakup of the USSR and of Yugoslavia, with German reunification or with the independence of Eritrea. They nonetheless reveal how relatively small an industrial power the former USSR, let alone Yugoslavia, was, and how sharply the industrial power of East Germany had been declining during the 1980s. German reunification itself demonstrated how hollow much industrial production in East Germany was, as state enterprises unable to compete effectively in world markets were either abandoned or modernized at enormous cost in new investment. In Russia, as in other successor states of the USSR, much of the industrial economy is now little more than a matter of stage management. And, meanwhile, industrial growth in some Asian states has been continuing apace.

35 PRODUCT POWER

In 1992, the value of exported goods worldwide totalled U.S. $3.73 trillion, almost double the 1982 total of U.S. $1.88 trillion.

Asian states have shown the most dramatic increases in exports, and their economies have thrived on a combination of relatively cheap labour and a high rate of investment in technology, skills and initiative. Hong Kong and Singapore have promoted a large trade in re-exports – goods which are imported and then, without being transformed, profitably exported again. In 1992, Hong Kong's trade in re-exports amounted to 75 percent of its total trade in exported goods.

The steep decline in the world market price of oil had a corresponding impact on those states for which oil is their paramount export. Bahrain, Ecuador, Gabon, Qatar, Trinidad and Tobago would have featured in a 1982 version of this cartogram but they do not feature ten years later. Bulgaria, which is among those states whose economies imploded with the collapse of the USSR, is absent; so, too, is Iraq, a state subject to international economic sanctions.

36 SERVICE POWER

In 1992, the value of worldwide exports in commercial services totalled U.S. $1 trillion, or well over double the total in 1982. Even so, the recorded statistics significantly understate their real value. Some transactions, such as the repatriated earnings of migrant workers, may be excluded as remittances; others defined as trade in goods rather than in services; and more importantly, still others, transmitted electronically, often go unrecorded, especially when they are transactions between parent companies and their foreign affiliates. It is a sector in which the sale of information, banking and other financial services, including insurance, is a particularly fast growing element of the world economy. This explains why the dominance of the U.S.A., with 16.2 percent of the world total, is even more marked than it is for the trade in goods, where it is 12 percent. The share of France, at 10.2 percent is also markedly larger than its share of the trade in goods, at 6.3 percent.

37 SCIENCE POWER

In the world of cyberspace, Internet and e-mail, not everyone would choose to measure science output by the number of articles published in learned journals, or gauge the influence of a scientific observation by the number of references to an article in subsequent journal articles. But the scientists themselves do so, and we have no option but to follow them.

The measure imparts a number of biases to the results: English-language publications score better than publications in other languages; Latin script is favoured over others; disciplines with a few major journals (physics and earth sciences, or engineering and technology, for example) fare better than those with a relatively dispersed literature (biology and mathematics).

The conclusion is nonetheless clear: whatever the measurement used, citations, articles or royalties and fees, the U.S.A. is the science superpower, Japan is a rapidly rising sun, and there is a small cluster of European contenders.

38 MILITARY POWER

The Cold War may be over but arms spending still gobbles up a tenth of all government expenditure worldwide. More than two-fifths of the total is spent by the U.S.A. Military spending is as shrouded in secrecy and arbitrary pricing as it always has been. China's declared military budget of U.S. $6 billion a year, for example, could be anything between U.S. $28.5 billion and U.S. $45 billion in reality, depending on the method of calculation.

39 UNDER ARMS

The end of the Cold War in 1989 inaugurated a wonderful period for war-mongers. Of the 136 states for which the comparison can be made, no fewer than 75, that is 55 percent, increased the size of their armed forces between 1985, when the Cold War was at its height, and 1994, the last year for which figures are available. Despite heavy reductions in some of the major military forces, in NATO and the countries of the former Warsaw Pact, the number of people under arms worldwide has increased by 36 percent, from 22 million to 30 million.

Included in the cartogram are all military servicemen and women on full-time duty; full-time active members of paramilitary forces whose training, organization, equipment and control suggest that they are used in support or in lieu of regular military forces; and active internal opposition forces that come into these categories. All Reserves are excluded, even in states such as Israel or Switzerland where they constitute a prime ingredient of military strategy. National guards are excluded as are civil defence forces, people's militias, secret services and all other covert and overt forces employed in safeguarding the security of the state. States whose armed forces amount to less than 0.01 percent of the world total are also excluded.

Some heavily militarized states make unusually heavy demands on their manpower by employing a large core of professionals in their conscripted armed forces.

40 STATE TERROR

States that resort to capital punishment or that promote, condone or simply do not expunge the use of assassination, 'disappearances', torture or other cruel, inhuman or degrading treatment are terrorist organizations – in the sense that they, often systematically, employ violence and the threat of violence to influence the behaviour of people unnamed or unknown.

State terror can be vicious, like Iran's or China's; it can be self-righteous like Israel's; or shamefaced like Australia's. States can be shedding the most gruesome aspects of their past as they are in Eastern Europe, Paraguay, and Mexico; or clinging to them as in Nigeria. Some use terror lavishly in the interests of its ruling groups, as in Iraq; others like Sweden, are minor players, which officially condemn it, occasionally condone it and seldom, if ever, prescribe it. There are some states where it is strictly rationed, as in the UK; and others where it is copiously available, as in India. And there are states in which the central authorities are blameless in intention but subverted by local government – Western Samoa or Bulgaria.

41 SMOKING GUNS

Many things make wars more likely and more destructive. Not least among them are the trade in arms and arms' accumulation. Although the Cold War has gone, hot wars proliferate. War itself is changing. In the early part of the 20th century, nine-tenths of war casualties wore uniform. This reflected the fact that most wars were between sovereign states, and were fought by trained men dedicated to the purpose. The prudent civilian could assume that he or she would be able to keep out of harm's way and survive the conflict.

This is no longer true. War is now primarily a domestic affair, waged between a state and its challengers. Civilian casualties outnumber military victims by nine to one. In most theatres of war, the prudent civilian wishing to survive would do well to join the armed forces.

The study of war cannot be an exact science. As the focus shifts from formal, structured, interstate conflicts waged by named agents with clear duties to record and report, to civil war, beginnings and ends become fuzzy. Casualty and refugee numbers become fuzzier. Judgement mingles with measurement, and definitional struggles colour reality. Is the person dying of cholera in a Rwandan refugee camp in Zaire a war casualty or a victim of disease? And what about the young woman scarred by multiple rape in Bosnia? Is she a casualty of war, or of something else?

42 REFUGEE MAKERS

Nobody knows how many people have been compelled to leave their homes for fear of persecution, injury or death, and would return if they could or dared. They must number hundreds of millions, huddled in the world's slums, swarming across frontiers and oceans, quarantined in special camps. Although they are fugitives from violence of one sort or another and from discrimination and deprivation, most of these people are not classed as refugees in the restricted sense employed by the agencies concerned with them.

To qualify as a refugee in that sense, a person must have crossed a recognized interstate boundary in his or her flight and also be in need of assistance and protection. Relatively few people satisfy both criteria.

Those that do qualify do not include the 'internally displaced': that is, refugees within their state's own frontiers. They do not include the vast mass in flight from destitution and debilitation; the growing army of 'asylum seekers' waiting for registration as 'real refugees'; the people in 'refugee-like circumstances' who are undocumented, unregistered or who, for some reason, fall outside the official protection mechanisms of host countries and international agencies; the forcibly relocated by government resettlement programmes; the small minority of 'real refugees who, welcome or not, miserable or desolate, have 'entered and resettled'; and people in a host of other categories and sub-categories.

The cartogram rests on a broader, though still restrictive, definition which includes as refugees 'asylum-seekers in need of assistance and/or protection' (that is, people 'unable or unwilling to repatriate due to fear of persecution and violence in their homelands or to be permanently settled in other countries') plus selected 'populations in refugee-like circumstances' plus the 'internally-displaced' and the 'forcibly located' (as given by the U.S. Committee for Refugees).

We have not included the vast array of fugitives who have stolen away rather than stampeded from trouble. Amongst them are the people who would not have left their homes in the first place and would almost certainly return if there were any hope there of elementary material security. These are the archetypal 'economic refugees': people forcibly returned in their thousands by the U.S. to Haiti, Cuba and Mexico, by the British (in Hong Kong) to Vietnam, by the Saudis to Ethiopia. They are the people forcibly blocked by Austria on its borders with the former Communist states of Eastern Europe; by Finland at its frontier with Russia; by Western Europe as a whole in its southern and eastern reaches; by Turkey on its border with Iraq.

We have also excluded the 'returnees': three-quarters of a million or so Russian 'Jews' to Israel; the one and a half million ethnic and not-so-ethnic Germans who trailed into the then Federal Republic in 1989 and 1990, the vast numbers who manage, against all odds, to get to their chosen destination without attracting attention – the multitudes of illegals in France, in Italy, in Spain, in the U.S.A. And then there are the officially 'entered and resettled'.

People who are displaced by accident or design are included only exceptionally. They are the victims of irrigation projects or other 'economic development' programmes, of industrial or 'natural' disasters, and more.

Refugees are created. In a world of states, it is usually the state that creates them, primarily through war and the collateral effects of war, but also through forms of discrimination which amount to systematic violence, or through bad husbandry. It is for this reason that the cartogram reverses the conventional presentation by focussing on the source states rather than on asylum states.

No states are rushing to offer havens even to 'real refugees'. As refugees multiply, they find it increasingly difficult to go forth legally, let alone with a semblance of dignity. Recipient states resort to subterfuges which would be laughable if their consequences were not so tragic.

Amnesty International reports from France that an Algerian policeman and his young wife, who fled after receiving death threats from the 'armed Islamic movement', were refused refugee status on grounds that 'manifestly, they have nothing to fear from the Algerian state'.

In Belgium, lawyers representing detained asylum seekers, having obtained a court order requiring the government to give them 48 hours' notice of the date and time of appeal hearings, found themselves stymied by the minister of the interior who announced that he would fight this 'absurd decision' all the way on appeal and, if necessary, would bring in legislation to overturn it.

Even in the Netherlands, usually more humane than most, 35 Zairean refugees were on the point of being sent back to Togo because, the Dutch foreign ministry stated formally, it had been assured by the representative of the UN High Commissioner for Refugees in Lome, the Togolese capital, that it was safe enough for them to return there. The UNHCR has no representative in Lome.

Airlines face fines if they bring into a country people who do not have the required visa and travel documents. Many bona fide refugees do not have travel documents, and many states have imposed visa requirements with the express purpose of keeping refugees out. The British Refugee Council records the case of the Bosnian refugee who was unable to join his wife and children in Switzerland because he had no passport. Instead he went to the UK under a scheme for wounded or disabled Bosnians, but after twelve months he had still not been given refugee status, and his wife and children had not been allowed to join him. This is only one of thousands of Catch 22s.

43 DEBT JEOPARDY

Few governments seriously attempt to balance their books except when foreign exchange and credit markets require them to do so. In general, they spend more than they have the ability or the audacity to extract in taxes. The cost of servicing accumulated debts is the first charge on a government's resources: the higher the burden of debt, the lower the proportion of revenue available for everything else.

Poor states face double jeopardy. In periods of easy credit – notably, when the international banks were awash with money deposited by the oil rich states – they were encouraged to borrow from abroad huge sums in relation to their own resources. That much of this money may have been misappropriated or wasted does not make the accumulated burden of servicing and repayment any less exacting. Even if some of this debt had been rescheduled or cancelled, what remains is an often crippling charge on foreign earnings.

The scale of official development assistance to poor states reveals how little the rich states are ready to provide in relation to their riches.

44 FUNNY MONEY

Inflation, like taxation, is as certain as death. Indeed, it is increasingly a furtive form of tax, by which the state commands goods, services or credit for which it later pays in depreciated currency. Inflation is socially more iniquitous than taxation because its prime victims tend to be the most vulnerable, such as the elderly who rely on their savings; workers without the power to ensure that their wages keep pace with the rise in prices; and all those whose poverty allows them no means of coping. It is only the few with the necessary skills and financial resources who can take action to neutralize the process or even profit from it. In extreme but not uncommon cases – notably now among the successor states of the former USSR – inflation becomes hyperinflation, when money loses its value so fast that multitudes are reduced to destitution.

45 GOD AND CAESAR

Even unimpeachably secular states, which deal evenhandedly with all orthodox faiths or ideologies, profess values which shape their activities – the rule of law, belief as a matter for individual choice, and the individual as the ultimate repository of sovereignty. Most states are less reserved. They range from the secular in theory but partisan in practice, through the committed but tolerant, to the fundamentalist.

Some of them, such as the ones that profess 'Marxism-Leninism', like China, or extreme, mystical nationalism, like Myanmar, uphold beliefs which are not those of their people. Others, which seem to uphold the prevailing popular beliefs, do so only in the most general sense. In practice the governing classes profess a distinct variant of the prevailing belief, as in large parts of Latin America or the Middle East. The diffusion of a handful of world cults has resulted in a doctrinal tapestry, each varied enough to cover the most incompatible social and political purposes.

State beliefs have not been unaffected by recent shifts in world power. 'Marxism-Leninism' as an official doctrine, with its prophets, holy texts, licensed interpreters, shrines, rituals and sacraments, is in steep decline. Mystical nationalism, with a similar spiritual armoury, is on the rise. At a popular level, volatile social change, experienced as personal insecurity, has resulted in an unprecedented and continuing surge of fundamentalism characterized by God-sanctioned militancy, a search for alternative religious and political institutions (which is putting the current incumbents under growing pressure), and the pretence of working within an unbroken tradition.

Claims that are made about the number of adherents to a belief should be taken with a pillar of salt. Confessions of faith are made in response to someone else's demands, and are, like taxes, paid willy-nilly. But unlike taxes payment is made in spiritual currency and cannot easily be gauged. That being the case, this atlas has reluctantly followed the religious encyclopaedists who, for obvious reasons, assign to everyone – babes in arms and dodderers in bed included – a coherent system of beliefs. The result is that numbers and, by implication, the level of general commitment to conventional faiths are grossly overstated.

46 PROGRAMMED VIEWS

Television, with its cultural and often subliminal impact, may well be the most potent form of mass communication. Though regulated to provide so-called balanced comment in some countries, in others it is a critical instrument in manipulating opinion. In poor countries, where relatively few sets may be privately available, community sets or those installed in cafés and bars, greatly augment the number of viewers.

Radio remains everywhere a significant medium, and not only where television sets are scarce. In the U.S.A., for instance, radio has become a far more important medium for the expression of – mainly right-wing – political views, through hosted talk shows or stations.

Newspaper circulation depends on more than the mere extent of basic literacy, and in some poor countries – where the cost of buying a newspaper is beyond the means of all but a very few – the circulation rate per 1,000 of the population is so low that it is statistically recorded as zero. Yet even there, newspapers may be influential in affecting opinion within the elite. Elsewhere, and particularly in the advanced economies with more or less democratic systems of government, the press is still the most potent medium for the direct transmission of political influence.

47 THE THREE MONKEYS

There is a world of difference between sifting through opinions and information to find what might be apt for given circumstances or to make them digestible, and censorship – the outlawing of views and news by people dedicated to the task. The one is inseparable from social life, the other a naked exercise of social and political power.

Formally, most states renounced censorship when they adhered to the UN's Universal Declaration of Human Rights which, in Article 19, holds that 'Everyone has the right to freedom of opinion and expression; this right includes freedom to hold opinions without interference and to seek, receive and impart information and ideas through any media and regardless of frontiers.'

Declarations, of course, are one thing, and practice is another. States employ an array of instruments to suppress unwelcome opinion and prevent its dissemination: killings, kidnapping, disappearances; arrests, detention and imprisonment; dismissals, threats and harassment; restrictions on movement and expulsion; control of news agencies, setting of guidelines, favouritism, leaks, control of access, training of media staff, surveillance of press clubs, herding and corralling of journalists; disinformation; legislation, licensing, bans, expulsions; ownership; bribes; allocation of scarce resources including newsprint, frequencies, typewriters, advertising.

Standard targets for censorship include editors, producers, journalists, printers, writers, academics, human rights activists, political dissidents, and artists of every variety. And among a state's many justifications for censorship are the protection of innocents from unfair criticism, from defamation and from the invasion of privacy; the protection of the state or national security; the control of sedition; the protection of public health, public morals, public order; the preservation of a linguistic, cultural or public regime; the correction of media bias; and, the enforcement of contractual obligations.

The inset map covers prisoners of conscience as defined by Amnesty International: people detained for their beliefs, colour, sex, ethnic origin, language or religion who have not used or advocated violence, as well as people considered by Amnesty as possible prisoners of conscience. It includes conscientious objectors to military service, and prisoners adopted by International PEN. The data and judgements on which the map is based relate to the early 1990s. The anomalies reflect the times, and biases of our sources.

48 TONGUE-TIED

The queen of imperial languages is English, the nearest the world has come to a common tongue. By the mid-1980s English was claimed as their home language by more than 300 million people. Another 300 million or so used English as a second language, and a further 100 million used it fluently as a foreign language. This is an increase of 40 percent since the 1950s. Other estimates put the total number of English speakers, including people with a lower level of fluency, at over one billion, that is, well over a quarter of the world's teenage and adult population.

English is used as an official or semi-official language in over 70 states and has a prominent place in another 20. It is the premier language of books, newspapers, aviation and air traffic control, international business, academic conferences, science, technology, medicine, diplomacy, war, sports, international competitions, pop music and advertising. Over two-thirds of the world's scientists write in English. Three-quarters of the world's mail is written in English. Of all the information stored in electronic retrieval systems, 80 percent is stored in English. English-language radio broadcasts transmitted abroad are received by over 150 million people in 120 states. More than 50 million children study English as an additional language at primary school; and over 80 million study it at secondary level. (These figures exclude China where over 100 million people are thought to have tuned into the BBC Television English series 'Follow Me' at some time.) In any one year the British Council helps a quarter of a million foreign students learn English in various parts of the world. In the U.S.A., nearly half a million foreign students of English are registered every year. This dominance of English, and the other imperial languages, effectively squeezes out indigenous languages, as is shown on Map 49 Pressures.

The main map greatly exaggerates the linguistic power of the world's population. Language can be a barrier as well as a bridge. Although there are many people for whom the dominant language is not a mother tongue (or home language) yet who can use it fluently and so participate fully in public affairs, there are very many more who claim the ruling language as theirs and yet, by reason of poor education, narrow experience or inadequate nurturing, use it so uncomfortably or in such a distinctive form as to be excluded from effective participation.

In the case of some ex-colonial states it is not always easy to know the real status of an indigenous second official language. Whether its speakers have access to 'rule' depends partly on the extent to which the language is taught at school, on the prevalence of literacy, or on some such shoehorn factor. In all cases the indigenous language has been given the benefit of the doubt.

49 PRESSURES

Some states use the law to secure conformity with proclaimed norms of sexual expression. Others rely on social pressure and prevailing attitudes. In many states, self-appointed guardians exert their own pressures through more violent methods.

We have classified states according to broad categories. 'Not forbidden by law' means only that there are no discriminatory provisions against homosexuality. It does not imply an absence of pressures through social disapproval. 'Legal with some discriminatory provisions' encompasses lawfulness but with such restrictions as a higher age of consent for homosexual than for heterosexual practices; the banning of homosexuality in a particular sector, usually the armed forces; and/or the specific banning of anal intercourse between men. 'Lawful but repressed' is a category applied to states where the law is silent on homosexuality, but provisions against 'indecency' or other formulations are effectively directed against homosexuals; where the harassment of homosexuals by the police or vigilantes is evidently sanctioned by the authorities; and/or the social climate is extremely hostile. 'Unlawful but tolerated' means that the authorities seldom prosecute and that society is largely tolerant (though in some such cases, the rise of fundamentalism is beginning to threaten the traditional attitude). The two remaining categories need no elaboration.

Less proscriptive but even more potent is the pressure exercised by the dominant culture on minority ones, and especially on the languages involved. Minority languages are everywhere under threat, not least from the few languages spoken internationally (see Map 48 Tongue-tied). The American Association for the Advancement of Science conference at Atlanta in February 1995 was informed that only ten percent of the world's 6,000 languages are likely to survive the next 100 years. Already between 20 percent and 50 percent are no longer being learned by children and will die with their surviving speakers.

50 ADDITION AND DIVISION

And still they come. Since the last edition of this atlas was being prepared, in 1990, 23 new states have raised their flags and posted ambassadors abroad. Most of them joined the United Nations.

The nation state is one in which, ideally, the political unit coincides with a popular sense of common identity. It goes no farther back than the 18th century. Of the states that exist today, only 14 have had an uninterrupted existence for more than 200 years. From 660 BC, when Japan came into being as a recognizable entity, to 1776, with the constitution of the U.S.A., these pre-19th century states came into being on average once every 175 years. Then the pace of state formation accelerated: to an average of one state every four years in the 19th century (28 in all), one in every 18 months in the first half of the 20th century (37 in all), one in every five months in the latter half of the 20th century, up to 1993 (105 in all).

It is not hard to understand why the novelty of the nation state was taken up so widely and with such profound effect. The emerging market system needed the state to underpin it. So rest assured that San Marino (population 24,091, area 60 kms^2) joined the UN on 2 March 1992, as did Liechtenstein (population 30,281, area 160 kms^2) on 18 September 1990, alongside the successor states to the USSR and Yugoslavia. In March 1995, there were 184 internationally recognized states (not including those recognized by only one other state, such as the Turkish Republic of Northern Cyprus).

Some of the new states are reincarnations of older ones: many of the 1990s crop are successor states to the former USSR and Yugoslavia. Some are waiting in the wings: in Israel or Morocco, for example, where they are restrained by forced possession, or in Sudan, Somalia or Liberia, where they are hatching in conflict with each other. For others – Canada, Spain, India, Indonesia perhaps – the bonds that hold the current states together are fraying. True, there are states and territories on a different trajectory: Hong Kong and Taiwan moving towards China, the Koreas towards unification. But appearances may well prove deceptive. Few of them enjoy the favourable circumstances of Germany, which was re-united in October 1990.

Ahooja-Patel, Krishna 'Gender Distance among Countries' *Economic and Political Weekly*. Bombay. February 1993.

Amnesty International (AI). *Conscientious Objection to Military Service*. London: AI, January 1991.

Amnesty International. *Report*. London: AI, annual.

Barrett, David B. ed. *World Christian Encyclopedia: A Comparative Study of Churches and Religion in the Modern World, AD 1900-2000*. Nairobi, Oxford and New York: Oxford University Press, 1982.

Belfield, Richard, Christopher Hird and Sharon Kelly. *Murdoch: The Great Escape*. London: Warner Books, 1994.

Borders and Territorial Disputes. 3rd ed. Harlow, Essex: Longman, 1992.

Central Intelligence Agency (CIA). *World Factbook 1993* and *1994*. Washington, D.C.: CIA, 1993 and 1994.

Europa Regional Yearbooks. London: Europa Publications, various dates.

Europa World Yearbook 1993. London: Europa Publications, 1994.

General Agreement on Trade and Tariffs (GATT). *International Trade Statistics 1993*. Geneva: GATT, 1994.

Greenpeace International. *Climate Time Bomb*. Amsterdam: Greenpeace, 1994.

Grimes, Barbara F. ed. *Ethnologue: Languages of the World*. 11th ed. Dallas, Texas: Summer Institute of Linguistics, 1988.

Gunnemark, Erik V. *Countries, Peoples and Their Languages*. Gothenburg: The Geolinguistic Handbook, n.d. (early 1990s).

Hungarian Academy of Sciences. *Scientometrics*. Budapest: Akademiai Kiado; and Amsterdam, Oxford, New York and Tokyo: Elsevier Science BV, serial 1994.

Index on Censorship. London: (monthly).

International Boundaries Research Unit (IBRU). *Boundaries and Security Bulletin*. Durham: University of Durham, Department of Geography, serial.

International Confederation of Free Trade Unions (ICFTU). *Free Labour World*. Brussels: serial.

International Institute for Strategic Studies (IISS). *The Military Balance 1993-94*. and *1994-95*. London: Brassey's, 1993 and 1994.

International Labour Office (ILO). *Yearbook of Labour Statistics*. Geneva: ILO, annual.

International Monetary Fund (IMF). *Economic Reviews* for Kirgistan, Tajikistan, Uzbekistan, 1992; Armenia, Azerbaijan, Georgia, Kazakhstan, Turkmenistan, Ukraine, 1993. Washington, D.C.: IMF, relevant dates.

International Monetary Fund (IMF). *Government Finance Statistics Yearbook 1993*. Washington, D.C.: IMF, 1993.

International Monetary Fund (IMF). *World Economic Outlook*. Washington, D.C.: IMF, October 1993.

International PEN. *Writers in Prison Committee, Case List, January 1994*. London: International PEN, 1994.

International Road Federation. *World Road Statistics 1953* and *1988-92*. Geneva: International Road Federation, 1953.

Keesing's Record of World Events. Harlow: Essex: Longman, serial.

Kurian, George Thomas. *Encyclopedia of the Third World*. New York and Oxford: Facts on File, 1992.

McEvedy, Colin and Richard Jones. *Atlas of World Population History*. London: Allen Lane, 1978.

Marty, Martin E. and R. Scott Appleby. eds. *Fundamentalisms and the State: Remaking Politics, Economics and Militance*. Chicago: Chicago University Press, 1993.

Marty, Martin E. and R. Scott Appleby. eds. *Fundamentalisms Observed*. Chicago: Chicago University Press, 1993.

Minority Rights Group. *World Directory of Minorities*. Harlow, Essex: Longman, 1989.

Motor Industry of Great Britain. *World Automotive Statistics 1993*. London: Society of Motor Manufacturers and Traders, 1993.

National Science Foundation (NSF). *Science and Engineering Indicators 1993.* Washington, D.C.: USGPO, 1993.

News Corporation. Annual Report, 1993.

Nicolaides-Bouman, A.N.S. and Nicholas Wald, with Barbara Forey and Peter Lee. eds. *International Smoking Statistics.* London: Institute of Preventative Medicine; and Oxford, New York and Tokyo: Oxford University Press, 1993.

O'Brien, Joanne and Martin Palmer. *The State of Religion Atlas.* London and New York: Simon and Schuster, 1993.

Parekh, Bhiku. 'Some Reflections on the Hindu Diaspora'. *New Community.* Coventry, University of Warwick, Centre for Research in Ethnic Relations. July 1994.

Population Action International. *Expanding Access to Safe Abortion: Key Policy Issues.* Washington, D.C.: PAI, September 1993.

Population Action International. *World Access to Birth Control.* Washington, D.C.: PAI, September 1992.

Population Concern. *1993 World Population Data Sheet.* London: Population Concern, 1994.

Population Reference Bureau. *1993 World Population Data Sheet.* Washington D.C.: Population Concern, 1993.

Privatisation International. *Privatisation Yearbook.* London: Privatisation International, annual.

Republic of China (Taiwan). *Statistical Yearbook 1993.* (Taipei) Directorate-General of Budget, Accounts and Statistics, 1993.

Russia and Eurasia: Facts and Figures. 18. Florida, Academic International Press, 1993.

Segal, Ronald. *The Black Diaspora.* London: Faber & Faber; New York: Farrar, Straus & Giroux, 1995.

Shawcross, William. *Rupert Murdoch.* London: Chatto & Windus, 1992.

Sivard, Ruth Leger. *World Military and Social Expenditures 1993.* Washington, D.C.: World Priorities, 1993.

Smith, Dan. 'Dynamics of Contemporary Conflict: Consequences for Development Strategies' in Nina Greager and Dan Smith. eds. *Environment, Poverty, Conflict.* Oslo: International Peace Research Institute (PRIO), 1994.

Staple, Gregory C. ed. *Telegraphy 1993: Global Telecommunications Traffic Statistics and Commentary.* Washington, D.C.: Telegeography Inc., 1993.

Statesman's Year Book 1993-94. London: Macmillan, 1993.

Stockholm International Peace Research Institute (SIPRI). *SIPRI Yearbook 1993: World Armaments and Disarmament.* Oxford and New York: Oxford University Press, 1993.

Tielman, Rob and Hans Hammelburg. 'World Survey on the Social and Legal Position of Gays and Lesbians' in Aart Hendriks, Rob Tielman and Evert van der Veen. eds. *The Third Pink Book.* Buffalo, New York: Prometheus Books, 1993.

Union Postale Universelle. *Statistique des services postaux 1992.* Berne: Bureau International de l'Union Postale Universelle, 1993.

United Kingdom 1991 Census of Population. *Research and Statistics.* London: Department of the Home Office, 1991.

United Nations. *Energy Statistics Yearbook 1991 and 1992.* New York: UN, 1991 and 1992.

United Nations. *Monthly Bulletin of Statistics.* March 1994. New York: UN, 1994.

United Nations. *World Investment Report 1993: Transnational Corporations and Integrated International Production.* New York: UN, 1993.

United Nations Children's Fund (UNICEF). *The Progress of Nations 1994.* New York: UNICEF, 1994.

United Nations Development Programme (UNDP). *Human Development Report 1994.* New York and Oxford: Oxford University Press, 1994.

United Nations Educational, Scientific and Cultural Organization (UNESCO). *Statistical Yearbook 1993.* Paris: UNESCO, 1993.

United Nations Environment Programme (UNEP). *Environmental Data Report 1993-94*. Oxford: Blackwell, 1993.

United Nations Industrial Development Organization (UNIDO). *Industry and Development Global Report 1993-94*. Vienna: UNIDO, 1993.

United States Arms Control and Disarmament Agency (USACDA). *World Military Expenditures and Arms Transfers 1991-92*. Washington, D.C.: USCR, annual.

United States Committee for Refugees (USCR). *World Refugee Survey*. Washington, D.C.: USCR, annual.

United States Department of Agriculture (USDA). *Tobacco: World Markets and Trade*. Washington, D.C.: USDA, 1994.

United States House of Representatives Committee on Energy and Commerce, Subcommittee on Telecommunications and Finance. Transcript of Hearing on Derivatives, 19 May 1994.

United States State Department. *Country Reports on Human Rights Practices for 1993*. Washington, D.C.: USGPO, 1994.

Universal Postal Union (UPU). *Postal Statistics 1992*. Berne: UPU, 1994.

Wallensteen, Peter and Karin Axell. 'Conflict and Resolution and the End of the Cold War'. *Journal of Peace Research*. 31(3) August 1994. London, Newbury Park and New Delhi: SAGE Publications (for PRIO).

World Bank. *Atlas 1994*. Washington, D.C.: World Bank, 1994.

World Bank. *The Environmental Data Book*. Washington, D.C.: World Bank, 1993.

World Bank. *Social Indicators of Development 1994*. Baltimore and London: Johns Hopkins University Press, 1994.

World Bank. *World Development Report 1993*. Washington, D.C.: World Bank, 1994.

World Bank. *World Tables 1992*. Baltimore and London: Johns Hopkins University Press, 1992.

World Directory of Diplomatic Representation. London: Europa Publications, 1992.

World Energy Council. *Report 1993: International Energy Data*. London: World Energy Council, 1993.

World Resources Institute. *World Resources 1991-92* and *1994-95*. New York and Oxford: Oxford University Press, 1992 and 1994.

World Tourist Office (WTO). *Yearbook of Tourism Statistics 1993*. Madrid: WTO, 1993.

In addition, we have been greatly helped by personal communications, not all of them cited in the acknowledgements on page 11; by press reports, principally in *The Economist* (in particular, of 16 March 1994), *Financial Times* (in particular, of 20 October 1993, 2 December 1993, 7 January 1994), *The Guardian* (in particular, of 25 June 1994, 1 August 1994, 20 February 1995), and *The Independent* (in particular, of 15 May 1994); and by press releases and database searches, notably from GATT, WHO and WTO.